Educating for Global Responsibility

Teacher-Designed Curricula
for Peace Education, K–12

Educating for Global Responsibility

Teacher-Designed Curricula
for Peace Education, K–12

Edited by

Betty A. Reardon

TEACHERS COLLEGE PRESS

Teachers College, Columbia University
New York and London

Published by Teachers College Press, 1234 Amsterdam Avenue,
New York, NY 10027

Library of Congress Cataloging-in-Publication Data

Educating for global responsibility.

  Bibliography: p.
  Includes index.
  1. Peace – Study and teaching (Elementary) – United
States.   2. Peace – Study and teaching (Secondary) –
United States.   I. Reardon, Betty.
JX1904.5.E377   1988   327.1′72′07073   87-18017

ISBN 0-8077-2879-9

Manufactured in the United States of America

93   92   91   90   89   88   1   2   3   4   5   6

Education can be defined as working with people, young and old, to prepare them to live in the future. The future may be bright. It may be gray. But, most importantly, we must ensure that *there will be a future.*

WILLARD J. JACOBSON
"Education for Peace"
Second Annual Nuclear Issues Conference
New York, February 1984

This book is dedicated to classroom teachers everywhere whose day-by-day struggle to ensure that there will be a future was the inspiration that produced it.

Contents

Acknowledgments

This collection results from a survey of teacher-designed peace education curricula made possible by the World Policy Institute under a grant from Mr. Earl D. Osborn, who recognizes the significance of elementary and secondary education in the overall effort to achieve world peace. His support over the years of many innovative and ground-breaking projects has made an invaluable contribution to the development of peace education.

The opportunity for Teachers College to carry out the project was provided by support from the Ira and Miriam Wallach Foundation for the initiation and development of the Peace Education Program. Mr. and Mrs. Wallach's emphasis on the need for university programs in peace and world order studies has resulted in the increased attention of this and other graduate schools of education to the preparation of teacher educators in this field.

The project that produced this book was carried out during 1984–1985 as a cooperative effort involving Ms. Barbara Wien, Director of Education for the World Policy Institute, and the Teachers College research team, which consisted of graduate students in the Peace Education Program— Gregory Leeds, Andrea Kimmich-Keyser, William Paringer—and the author, who is the director of the Program. The survey was distributed by the World Policy Institute, and the curriculum materials were gathered and analyzed by the team from the Teachers College Peace Education Program. It was a satisfying and stimulating task to work with all four of them, and I am grateful to them for a very rewarding teaching/learning experience.

The third sponsor of the guide is the Peacemaking in Education Program of United Ministries in Education, whose support and endorsement of the project made it possible for the author to coordinate the research and draft of the manuscript.

Deep appreciation is also extended to Willard Jacobson and Douglas Sloan, my colleagues at Teachers College who have collaborated in the building of the Peace Education Program. This collaboration has afforded me a rich experience of learning and friendship.

Thanks, too, to Robert Schwarz and the staff of the Teachers College Word Processing Center; their caring, careful, and prompt deciphering of the script for this manuscript was an enormous help.

Most special and affectionate thanks go to Willard Jacobson, my doctoral advisor, who started me on this phase of my peace education endeavors and supported and guided me through it.

Finally, I want to express admiration and thanks to the many classroom teachers whose work provides the curricular bases of this book. Theirs is the credit for the real work of peace education in the schools of this country. I hope the book will be a help to them and to those who follow in their footsteps. I trust, too, that I have been able to maintain the integrity of their efforts in the formulation they are given here. Any misinterpretations or inappropriate formulations are the sole responsibility of the author and compiler.

Foreword

This collection of elementary and secondary peace education curricula is a unique effort for the World Policy Institute. For the last decade the Institute's efforts have been concentrated in the areas of world order research and university program development. In my years as Director of Academic Outreach at WPI, it became clear to me that there was a real need for pre-collegiate peace education and equally clear that there was much creative work being done by classroom teachers. My experience in collecting and editing the university curricula published in the Fourth Edition of *Peace and World Order Studies* led me to believe that a similar volume for K–12 would produce a positive response from peace educators. My belief was shared by Mr. Earl Osborn, who made it possible for me to initiate the survey whose results are published here.

The responses of classroom peace educators substantiated my belief and fulfilled Mr. Osborn's vision of creating a tool for the introduction of peace education into elementary and secondary schools across the country. We both appreciate the efforts of the Teachers College team and the creativity and commitment of the teachers who responded to our call for curricula. We hope that this collection will be only the first of many similar efforts to develop peace education in grades K–12.

BARBARA J. WIEN
Institute for Policy Studies
formerly
Director of Academic Outreach
Program, World Policy Institute

Introduction: Education to Ensure a Future

The whole of human society is faced with the challenge of making global policy choices that will determine whether or not our species will survive. Education must therefore face up to the need to prepare the young for global responsibility, to understand the nature and implications of global interdependence, and to accept the responsibility to work for a just, peaceful, and viable global community on planet Earth. Every person inhabiting the planet bears some responsibility to contribute to the resolution of the problems that constitute this unprecedented challenge to the human family. Education must help every student to develop a global identity and a planetary perspective as a framework with which to confront the survival issues we face. Three major problems threaten the future of the planet and the well-being of humanity: the population/poverty dynamic, environmental/ecological crises, and war and nuclear weapons. All three of these interrelated global problems are included within the purview of peace education as it is interpreted by the teachers represented in this collection of peace education curricula. They are most notably reflected in three fundamental value concepts found throughout peace education efforts of all kinds as they are currently practiced: positive human relationships based on the dignity of all persons; stewardship of planet based on a reverence for the Earth; and global citizenship based on responsibility to a world community. These values sum up the most general notions of what comprises global responsibility in the eyes of most peace educators. They are the fundamental criteria for planetary policy making, if we are to "ensure that there will be a future."

In the last several years, the recognition of the urgency of peace issues has led to a quantum leap in the attention given to education for peace and the prevention of nuclear war, and for the improvement of the quality of human life and of the global environment. This leap was impelled by educators struggling to provide their students with a legitimate hope in the future of the Earth, and by the efforts undertaken by classroom teachers, singly, in faculty groups, and sometimes in organizations. Over the past few decades, growing numbers of classroom teachers have been developing their own curricula related to questions of global responsibility, peace, and justice in general, and more recently and more numerously on nuclear weapons and nuclear war in particular. It has been largely through the efforts of many of these teachers that a major national organization, Educators for Social Responsibility (ESR), came into being. So, too, it was the concern and the persuasion of teachers in association with the like-minded national staff that combined to make the issue of nuclear weapons a central concern of the National Education Association (NEA). The bulk of this book is the work of such teachers.

The two national organizations, ESR and NEA, have published major collections of curriculum material (see *Dialogue* and *Choices* in Recommended Curriculum Materials). These are not the only materials available, however; a variety of others, albeit less well known, have been developed by research agencies, international organizations, peace groups, and religious denominations. Notable among these is *Repertoire of Peacemaking Skills* (see Recommended Curriculum Materials), published by the Consortium on Peace Research, Education, and Development (COPRED). Nevertheless, the preparation of most peace education materials is still being done by classroom teachers, who devise their own courses and units. Additional materials may be found in the listings and libraries of resource centers such as the Peace Education Resource Center at Teachers College. There is a growing, varied, and rich pool of materials for peace education, K–12.

The main purpose of this collection of teacher-designed peace education curricula is to demonstrate within the narrow limits of these few selections the wide range of possibilities for integrating peace education into all areas of the curriculum at all grade levels, and to encourage systematic efforts in curriculum development for a comprehensive approach to peace education (Reardon, 1988). Another purpose is to serve some of the immediate needs of teachers for peace education curriculum examples, to encourage them to study the field more deeply, and to provide an impetus for further study and research in curricular needs in the field that can lead to the development of a comprehensive, integrated curricular program for K–12 peace education in all of the nation's schools.

The initial motivation for producing this guide was the need for readily available peace education curriculum material in a form easily adaptable by classroom teachers seeking to initiate courses or units in peace education. Since classroom teachers themselves, as noted above, are the primary source of such material, the national survey mentioned in the Acknowledgments was conducted to gather teacher-designed curricula on the three major global problem areas. Many of these curricula had been tested and refined over several years of use. A compendium of selections extracted from some of the materials gathered in the survey is offered here as an initial attempt to help meet some of the growing curricular needs of a rapidly developing field.

It is hoped that this curriculum collection will be an encouragement to many more teachers and school systems to begin programs, develop courses, or introduce units, and that it will reinforce the efforts of other agencies working in the field, many of which assisted in the survey by publishing notices in their newsletters and by providing mailing lists.

The work of these agencies has been a significant impetus to the field; so, too, was the recent rash of state and local mandates and guidelines calling for the introduction of the study of nuclear weapons and conflict into the public schools. These statements, an encouragement to this project, followed the trend set in motion by the U.S. Office of Education in its 1968 Statement on Needs and Priorities in International Education, a trend manifested on an international scale by the 1974 UNESCO Recommendation on Education for International Understanding, Cooperation, and Peace and Education Concerning Human Rights and Fundamental Freedoms, which defines and outlines the field within parameters as broad as its title is long. The principles and guidelines offered by those ground-breaking statements are reflected in many of the selections in this book and provide a sound basis for the development of the much-needed comprehensive program.

By far the strongest encouragement was the response of K–12 peace educators to the announcement of the project. More than 130 curricula were received, ranging from short units of several pages to complete courses with all the component materials. All of these materials are on deposit in the Milbank Memorial Library Curriculum Resource Center at Teachers College, Columbia University, where they may be used by peace educators. A description of each curriculum is also entered into a computer-based "Peace Education Curriculum Bank" that is to be made accessible on a nationwide basis.

The Selection Process

The selection of curricula for inclusion in the guide was made according to a set of criteria developed by the research team. Each submission was individually assessed by every member of the team on the basis of the following ten criteria.

1. The conceptual clarity with which the central ideas and topics were expressed and described.
2. The conceptual and structural relationships among and between the component parts, the degree to which the curriculum was a well-integrated whole.
3. Clear and specific learning objectives conceptually related to peace

education, which could be demonstrated by students and observed by teachers.

4. A relationship between the designated learning objectives and the proposed instructional methods that assures the suitability of the teaching means to the learning ends.

5. A relationship among the objectives, methods, and topics that reflects conceptual clarity and assures appropriateness of the instructional media to the learning goals.

6. Appropriateness of the curricula to the designated learners, indicating careful review of the needs and capacities of the learners and relevance of the topics and methods to both the specific grade and subject as well as to peace education.

7. An evident relationship between the topics and objectives and the learning requirements for achieving peace (i.e., peacemaking).

8. Reliability and accuracy of the substantive content of the curriculum.

9. Applicability of the curriculum to other learning settings in other communities, with different groups of students.

10. The curriculum is presented so as to be readily adaptable and usable by other teachers.

These criteria were formulated not only to make the selections for this guide, but also to provide some general standards that teachers and curriculum coordinators can apply to selecting the most useful materials from the growing array of curricula on peace and the other survival issues. Another very useful tool for assessing peace education curricula is "Ten Quick Ways to Evaluate Peace Education Materials" prepared by the Peace Education Network (PEN) and available from COPRED (see Resource Organizations).

Even with these qualitative standards, selection was a difficult process. All the material submitted had merit, but some met the standards more fully than others. Choosing which specific extracts to include was also difficult. They were generally chosen so as to provide variety of subject matter and to reveal as many characteristics and aspects of peace education as possible. The entries as a whole demonstrate that peace education can be integrated into all subjects at all grade levels. The extracts attempt to demonstrate the breadth of the field while offering short, specific, replicable units that teachers can readily adapt without extensive additional preparation. It is hoped, however, that all who use this book will want to deepen their knowledge of the field and become more familiar with more of the curricula now available. For this reason, an annotated bibliography of selected commercially published curricula is included as an appendix. A bibliography of selected theoretical works may be found in *Comprehensive Peace Education: Educating for Global Responsibility* (Reardon, 1988), a companion to this guide.

The Conceptual Content of Peace Education

There are as yet no clear and precise limits to nor standards for what is to be included in peace education. The survey revealed that a wide variety of topics and teaching techniques were seen by classroom teachers as appropriate to education for peace, justice, and a healthy global environment. For the purposes of preparing this guide, the research team accepted the definitions of subject matter and instructional methods proposed by the teachers who sent in their curricula. The topics were reviewed and categorized several times. Ultimately the following topics were identified as the general conceptual areas currently included in the field. These topics also serve as the substantive categories for computer indexing the ongoing collection of curricular materials at Teachers College.

Peace (Concepts, Models, Processes)
Conflict, Conflict Management, Conflict Resolution, War, Weapons
Cooperation and Interdependence
Nonviolence (Concepts, Practices, Cases)
Global Community, Multicultural Understanding, Comparative Systems
World Order, Global Institutions, Peacekeeping (Methods, Models, and Cases), Alternative Security Systems
Human Rights, Social Justice, Economic Justice, Political Freedom
Social Responsibility, Citizenship, Stewardship, Social and Political Movements
Ecological Balance, Global Environment, World Resources

Throughout the materials the central value concepts — stewardship, citizenship, and relationship — appear as the fundamental core concepts that govern both curriculum content selection and design and the choice of which issues are to be studied. In a sense teachers see these core values as the proper means of addressing the three major survival problems that humanity faces, and each relates to the central conceptual concern of peace education, *violence*, defined as unnecessary, avoidable harm to life and well-being.

Stewardship is expressed as the fundamental value to be developed as a response to the ecological crisis. Teachers are seeking to nurture in their students a new relationship to the planet, one based on an understanding of the life systems of the planet and how humans relate to them. They hope to develop a sense of caring for the living Earth and a desire to reverse the damage done by human interventions, especially those caused by war, weapons testing, and irresponsible development. In sum, the value calls for reversing the violence inflicted on the natural environment.

The *relationship* binding together all the peoples of the Earth in a network of interdependence is also central to peace education, particularly those efforts that deal with poverty and development and cross-cultural understanding. Peace educators hope to develop in their students attitudes and capacities that will foster a system of positive human interdependence based on a respect for human dignity and universal human rights. The value calls attention to the violence inherent in social, economic, and political structures that impede the realization of human rights.

Citizenship in a global society requires the acquisition of new skills as well as the development of global and human values. If the problems of war and nuclear weapons are to be resolved, there must be an assumption of global responsibility on the part of individuals who see themselves as active citizens participating in a global community. Knowledge of the social and economic systems of states, approaches to international cooperation, and mechanisms for nonviolent conflict resolution are therefore featured content in many peace education programs. This value seeks the abolition of the violence of armed conflicts, particularly war.

These central value goals are reflected in most of the content and specific learning objectives identified in the curricula included here. Readers may wish to review other conceptual areas and other goals and objectives as described in some of the materials listed among the annotated resources. However, it is hoped that all who come into the field will reflect on these three fundamental value concepts and devise their own content and preferred learning objectives in the light of those concepts.

The General Learning Goals of Peace Education

The particular learning goals and objectives of current peace education practice are as varied as the topics and themes that derive from its central concepts. However, the fundamental purposes, like the conceptual bases of the curriculum, can be stated in general terms as overarching goals. The goals of resolving and transcending the major problems of war, poverty, and environment call for the development of a set of human capacities for the exercise of global responsibility. The peace educators who responded to the survey seemed to be striving for the development of three such general capacities: care, concern, and commitment.

The development of the capacity to care about the issues and problems of the world community and about the lives and well-being of all those who share our planet is the fundamental goal that underlies most of the affective objectives listed on the survey entry forms. The values and attitudes cited among the learning objectives were, for the most part, particular components of an ethic of care and the standards of justice which teachers held as the characteristics most to be desired in human relationships.

The capacity for concern, or the focusing of informed attention on the issues and problems, seems to be at the heart of what peace educators seek in their specific cognitive objectives: providing information and imparting skills for the analysis, evaluation, and application of information. While this capacity is primarily evident in cognitive objectives, it also serves to demonstrate that the realms of "thinking" and "feelings" are not totally separate one from the other. In pursuing the goals of peacemaking and peace education as preparation for peacemaking, an interweaving of values reflected upon and facts carefully examined is necessary if responsible action is to result.

Commitment is the capacity to sustain efforts toward bringing the results of study and reflection to bear on social and political activity. It forms the foundation of movements for social and political change and is the criterion by which education for empowerment is tested. Commitment to peacemaking as a fundamental civic obligation is the goal peace education espouses as primary in educating for global responsibility.

The Place of Peace Education in the Curriculum

There are virtually no subjects or grade levels for which peace education is not currently provided. However, there are many areas in which very sparse efforts are being made. While it is clear that much of the regular planned socialization of early childhood education and the primary grades is, in fact (although not self-consciously so), peace education, the survey revealed little intentionally designed programming at that level. It appears that programs and courses increase with grade level, and the highest concentrations therefore occur in senior high school, undoubtedly as a result of the recent growth in education related to nuclear weapons and global conflict.

Secondary level courses and units are taught as part of a social studies curriculum far more often than any other subject area, probably a reflection of the view that the questions under study are primarily issues of public policy that should be addressed within the realm of citizenship education. The subjects most frequently linked with social studies programs—English and language arts—are also the areas with the second greatest concentration of peace education programs. We found lamentably few programs or units in science, mathematics, and the arts. It should be noted, however, that some science programs in environment education that are not intentionally peace education, such as those in early childhood, may in fact be consistent with the content and purposes of education for stewardship. However, the survey revealed only a very few designated as peace education programs. It is thus very important that the subject areas of the arts and sciences be stressed in further curriculum development for peace education.

There are two general approaches to integrating peace education into the current curricula: introduction of specific new content and infusion of existing content.

Curricula in specific subject areas reflect the fact that some peace education is offered as subject matter content, often as discrete units or particular courses. Such peace education emphasizes substance and cognitive learning about issues of peace. It reflects an assumption that the greatest need is particular cognitive knowledge regarding the issues and problems of peace and justice.

The other—and probably more widely practiced—approach is the infusion method. The assumptions underlying this method are that schools and teachers will be unwilling or unable to engage in extensive retraining or purchase of a significant amount of new material, and that the problems and issues of peace and justice are so pervasive that they cannot be adequately addressed with individual courses and units. The approach therefore is to infuse the entire curricular program—all grades, all subjects—with elements of peace and justice education. Teachers and students are introduced to a set of fundamental concepts (most of which are elaborations on the three central concepts) that are highlighted and explored by raising relevant questions within the context of existing curricula (see the description of the *Infusion Manual* in Recommended Curriculum Materials). Infusion is now widely used in Catholic secondary schools as the result of the one- to three-day workshops given throughout the country by the Justice and Peace Education Council (see Resource Organizations).

Although there is some debate over the comparative effectiveness of these two approaches, we believe both have a significant role to play in a comprehensive program of peace education, and we therefore advocate combining them whenever possible. This collection is an attempt to demonstrate that the development of such an approach starting from the basis of current materials and practices is certainly possible. It is offered as a first step toward such a process. We hope, too, that educators and citizens will undertake the development of locally based school programs involving teacher preparation and curriculum development. One possible approach to undertaking such efforts is outlined in *Militarization, Security and Peace Education* (Reardon, 1982), which also contains a schema for curriculum development.

The Organization of the Collection

This book is divided into sections based on grade levels and stages for the development of peacemaking capacities in elementary and secondary school students. The curriculum selections in each section can be used as presented, adapted, or combined with other materials in programs to develop peacemaking capacities. Each selection is preceded by a brief narrative highlighting particular concepts, objectives, or approaches especially significant to the development of these capacities, and each section opens with a set of comments on the general areas to be especially emphasized at that stage of development. The use of the term "we" in these comments refers to the research team of Leeds, Kimmch-Keyser, Paringer, and Reardon. The selections have been numbered and are referred to by number at various points in the commentary when examples of the concepts and purposes being emphasized are called for. It should be noted that these numbers correspond to the order in which the selections appear in this collection; the entry numbers under which these curricula are stored in the Teachers College Peace Education Curriculum Bank are not the same.

The first section is devoted to the stage of "early childhood." We recommend the materials included in this section for use in kindergarten through third grade with children aged 5–8, the stage at which children should first be introduced to the concept of peace and the notion of themselves as peacemakers. As it has become more customary for "formal" early childhood education to begin with preschoolers, many of the concepts and approaches recommended for this stage are also applicable to "nursery school" with children aged 2½–5, perhaps the most significant stage in the child's development of concepts of self and others.

The second section contains materials for "childhood." The materials here are suitable for Grades 4–6 (ages 9–11), when children should begin to develop a sense of social responsibility and are able to undertake more active roles as peacemakers both in their schools and in their communities. Some teachers of Grades 3 and 4 will doubtless find the material in the first section more suited to the children in their classes than those in the second section. There are likely to be cases in which materials and approaches for both stages can be adapted to Grades 3 and 4, depending on the developmental levels of individual children and of the class of general. We urge teachers of these and other transition grades at the beginning and end of each stage to review both relevant sections in making their selections.

Section three is devoted to the "pre-adolescence" stage and includes Grades 7 through 9 (ages 12–14). This is the stage at which more serious study of peace as a world problem can be initiated and the notion of institutional peacemaking and the responsibilities of global citizenship should be introduced.

Curricula for Grades 10 through 12 are presented in the last section as the "adolescence" stage (ages 15 through 17 or 18). It is to be hoped that students will emerge from secondary school as socially responsible young adults, well prepared to understand, take positions, and undertake action on global concerns, particularly issues of peace and justice, as they individually accept global responsibility.

Space does not allow us to reproduce most of the selections entirely as they were submitted to the survey. We have extracted segments from each curriculum on the basis of central concepts with a view to providing a sampling of as broad a range as possible of the current topics and approaches revealed by the survey to be of major significance to peace education as it is now practiced in American schools.

The entire curriculum from which each of these extracts was selected can be "called up" from the computer facilities of the Teachers College Peace Education Resource Bank, and from other computer systems with which it is to be interlinked. In addition to these and other unpublished curricula, the bank also contains reprints of key articles and sources in peace education not readily accessible in most libraries. Published curricula and the general literature of the field are also available in the Milbank Memorial Library of Teachers College and may be retrieved through the regular library indices. Readers wishing further information on accessing these and other resources may write to the Peace Education Program at Teachers College. It is our hope that a national network of such resource centers will be established.

We have reproduced information from the survey entry forms to assure that the original purposes and objectives of the authors of extracted curricula are properly described. Our selections and comments often narrow and specify these purposes to those we believe to be most relevant to a comprehensive, integrated approach to a total K–12 program for peace education.

Some selections are supplemented with references to similar or complementary materials and with suggestions for background reading. Most of these references are fully annotated at the end of this book in the sections on recommended curricula and bibliographies.

All of the materials here have been used in classrooms. While introductory remarks indicate the significant conceptual and theoretical aspects of the selections, actual prior application in age-appropriate learning settings was also a requirement for inclusion in this collection.

Readers will find that the materials are so varied in approach and content that they do not lend themselves well to categorization other than by grade level. Nevertheless, these selections clearly demonstrate that peace education can be conducted at every grade level and in every subject. Many teachers are now engaged in meeting the unprecedented professional challenge to educate for global responsibility. May the curriculum samples in this guide help many others to follow their lead, in the struggle to ensure that there will be a future.

Educating for Global Responsibility

Teacher-Designed Curricula
for Peace Education, K–12

SECTION I
The Early Grades (K–3)

Opening Up Peacemaking Capacities

There is no doubt that children enter school with attitudes about people and the world already formed by their experience as infants and toddlers. A truly comprehensive peace education would, in fact, begin with parent education (McGinnis & McGinnis, 1981). However, nursery school, kindergarten, and the primary grades are the first contact most children have with the larger society and the possibilities for peacemaking. The ages of 3 to 8 years are therefore crucial in developing peacemaking capacities. These grades will be very significant in how young children perceive strangers and others, how they feel about group and communal relations, and what they learn about relationships, caring, and cooperation. The role of the teacher may be more important at this first stage of the development of peacemakers than at any other.

Emotional and Aesthetic Capacities:
Toward Stewardship and Efficacy

The physical environment the teacher creates is vitally important to how children perceive and respond to the world around them. If they are surrounded by an aesthetically nourishing atmosphere, one that reflects care and appreciation of beauty, they can better learn to care for and appreciate the beauty of all environments, those of nature and those we invent and construct. If the emotional climate is loving and nurturant, reinforcing both the specialness and the equal value of all members of the group, the child will be better able to develop a sense of self-worth and a respect for others (see Selection 1). If learning is viewed as the way to increase our understanding of the world, ourselves, and others, then learning will be valued for its own sake and not as a tool for material gain. Cognition will become a means for personal fulfillment and community enrichment rather than a mechanism to control the environment and others. All of these elements combine into an atmosphere of mutuality essential to stewardship, in which education can truly bring forth new and hopeful possibilities, and open up chil-

1

dren's capacities not only for stewardship, but also for relationship, and citizenship.

One very significant capacity to awaken a sense of efficacy in the early grades is that of the creative imagination. Imagination is often released by guided imagery and meditation (see Selection 2). The skill of clearing the mind and relaxing the body in preparation for a task or as a respite during demanding activity can be developed in young children and can serve as the basis for the development of other peacemaking skills. Meditation has been used successfully in the early grades in various countries, most notably the Laboratory School of the University of Costa Rica (V. Rivera de Solis, personal communication, 1980). Its adherents maintain that the practice reduces tensions and releases energies for more effective learning, for increased creative activity, and for dealing constructively with conflict. It is also an excellent foundation for developing a whole range of reflective capacities seen as essential to peacemaking (Reardon, 1988).

Although themes of peace and justice that would *produce* fear clearly should not be introduced, a peace education sensitive to children's emotional needs must acknowledge the need to confront the fear that nuclear weapons, war, violence, and conflict can produce in children. Children should be encouraged to express their fears and to articulate and share the ways in which they cope with these fears (see Selection 2). This encouragement provides children with a greater sense of efficacy as their own coping abilities help them to become more secure. If empowerment is to be a goal of peace education, a sense of security and a repertoire of coping capacities must first be developed (see *Creating the Caring, Capable Kid* in Recommended Curriculum Materials).

Positive Self-Concept the Basis for Positive Human Relationships

Respect for self and others is the cornerstone of positive human relations, and its development should be critical to early childhood education. The peacemaking process is one that derives in large part from the concept of respect for others. Indeed, Benito Juarez, one of the great national heroes of Mexico, defined peace as "respect for the rights of others." Such respect is the essential requirement for the fulfillment of rights as they are defined in the Universal Declaration of Human Rights, for nonviolent conflict resolution, and for the fair negotiation of any human agreement or social contract. In short, unless sufficient value is placed on the rights of others, there is little likelihood of the achievement of positive peace. In turn, a respect for rights depends in large part on respect of the individual and cultural identity of others and on a positive perception of human differences. This respect

and perception need to be nurtured from the earliest years, certainly beginning with the first social experiences children have with others who are
different from them (see Selection 3).

Respect for Fairness and Order: Capacities for Citizenship

Children's most significant socialization usually takes place in the early
grades. It is in Grades 1 through 4 that most children have their first planned
experience with a social order, the classroom. It is here that they learn the
need for group regulation and procedures and where they begin to develop
the social skills of successful group membership. Thus it is in these grades
that the notion of individual responsibility for the maintenance of a peaceful and fair social order must be intentionally developed (see Selection 4).
The concept of peace as a dynamic, positive, nourishing social order should
be central to peace education for these years. So, too, should the development of a specific set of skills for responsible community action. Procedures
for developing these concepts and skills can be found in many early elementary peace curricula; however, these curricula are not without problems and
contradictions.

There is a delicate balance to be maintained if peace education is to
socialize children into a respect for law and communal order while at the
same time encouraging a sense of individual responsibility and a conscience
committed to justice. Not many curricula are sensitive to the problem of
achieving this balance and to the potential contradictions of these objectives. Some, it seems, may err somewhat on the side of emphasizing obedi-
ence to the detriment of conscience, consequently impeding a commitment
to justice and the changes needed to achieve it.

Teachers at this first stage (as at every stage) need to be clear about their
own assumptions and values, especially as they affect their teaching. The
examination of assumptions, an essential part of the exploration of all
approaches to peace, is particularly important in education for peace. Just
as students need to learn to examine assumptions that underlie opinions
about and proposals for peace, teachers need to become acutely aware of the
assumptions upon which curricula and teaching methods are based. The
close relationship between assumptions and values demands that teachers
examine teaching materials and techniques to gain a thorough understanding of all their intended purposes, which may be somewhat obscured by the
neutral language of learning objectives. So the formulation of learning
objectives must reflect a thorough examination of assumptions and values.

Thus, in the early grades, the curriculum should stress learning experiences that lay the foundation for the general capacities and particular skills

and attitudes characteristic of peacemakers. These experiences will profoundly influence children's capacities for positive human relationships, their notions of citizenship, and their attitudes toward the environment. Learning to value oneself and others, to respect differences, to trust and be trustworthy, and to appreciate the capacities of the human imagination, particularly its ability to find and make beauty in the world, is what we believe forms the essential early childhood foundation for a comprehensive, integrated peace education program. What follows are a few sample curricula that can be used to lay such a foundation.

The Learning Environment: The Fundamental Conditions for Peace Education

The two most important elements in the peace education process are: (1) the stance and style of the teacher, and (2) the learning environment. The environment is, for the most part, the result of the teacher's style. A learning environment has physical, emotional, and cognitive components, all of which derive from the values of the teacher, the school, the community, and the larger society; first and foremost among these sources, however, is the teacher's attitude toward the learners.

Creating a positive loving and human environment is Maureen Kushner's objective in her classroom in P.S. 132, a New York City elementary school attended primarily by low-income and minority youngsters. Ms. Kushner begins their school experience with exercises in community building and imagination. She helps them to see the positive and prophetic aspects of authentic heroism and the excitement and challenge of peacemaking. She demonstrates the dynamic, active nature of peacemaking and shows that what makes a hero is a person's willingness to struggle and sacrifice in all kinds of ways for the sake of a peaceful and just community. In this process she emphasizes two capacities essential for peacemaking, celebration and reconciliation, both of which need to be intentionally taught if children are to truly love life and strive to fulfill its promise. These capacities are the cornerstone of peacemaking. Most important of all, Kushner communicates to the children her own care and concern for them. By demonstrating that they matter to her, that they matter as persons, she teaches them to value themselves as well as their community.

We offer as our introduction to the early grade curricula excerpts from a proposal for a book describing her work. The publication of this entire book would serve a real need in peace education, describing the fundamental conditions necessary to the peacemaking classroom.

SELECTION 1
Dream-Makers, Peacemakers, and Heroes:
Teaching Old Values and New Visions

Entrant: Maureen Kushner
School: P.S. 132, Manhattan, 185 Wadsworth Avenue, New York, NY 10033
Grade Level: K–6
Department: Integrative
Concepts: Love, justice, truth, beauty, faith
Topics: Integrative
Materials: Assorted art materials and books; field trips.
Instructional Methods: Individualized reading and math; creative thinking;
     field trips.
Cognitive Objectives: The excellence of academic skills.
Affective Objectives: To integrate intuitive, spiritual, moral and aesthetic
     values into the elementary school curriculum; to encourage children to
     become dream-makers, peacemakers, and heroes; to create a beautiful/
     peaceful classroom environment.

OVERVIEW

Dream-Makers, Peacemakers, and Heroes describes the ways and techniques I have used to integrate intuitive, spiritual, moral, and aesthetic
values into the elementary school curriculum. This book explores imaginative methods that can be used to teach the importance of dream-making,
peacemaking, vision, and heroism to children and to create a cooperative,
beautiful, and peaceful environment in the classroom.

Children are being educated for the roles they will play in the communities in which they will later work and live. Since the classroom is their
immediate community, I try from the beginning to create an environment —
through good feelings, humor, beautiful images, stories, sounds, colors, and
forms — where children will look upon each other as sisters and brothers, as
good friends, as an extended family. I hope to help children learn how to
champion an ideal, follow through with commitment and skill, and communicate and inspire that ideal in others.

Our classroom is a collaboration based on the faith that it is natural for
people to create what is essential to them. We learn to trust our instincts, to
awaken our imagination, to act on our dreams, to create. We try together as
a class, both teacher and students, to create a common dream. Dream-
making is the spontaneous, propelling force; academic disciplines and art
are the language of our discoveries and understanding. We apply practical

skills to pursue our ideas. By developing peacemaking abilities, we learn to deal with injustices without resorting to violence.

The teaching project is elaborately developed during the year through a variety of activities. An original musical chant, motto, and logo are created for each project theme. The children produce murals and class books for every class project. There are approximately seven to ten celebrations during the year, each of which is based on subject matter and events connected to a particular theme. The teacher helps the children to conceive and organize each celebration. The celebrations are multi-media events combining drama, music, art, and ritual. At least three times a year a class fair is held to raise money for the celebrations and a social action project related to the class project is developed and carried out.

In the process of creating the celebrations, the children apply their academic skills and acquire the decision-making, listening, and social skills necessary for cooperative work. The children begin the year by choosing activities that they do best. Through an apprenticeship system, they expand their repertoire of skills by learning from their classmates, as well as from teachers, parents, and visitors to the class. The children form whatever committees are necessary for the creation of the celebration. These committees range in scope from the creative arts and administration to food preparation and public relations. The children appoint two peacemakers for each class, whom they consult when conflicts arise. The peacemakers in turn appoint two apprentice peacemakers, who will take over the role of peacemakers during the second half of the year.

Children are encouraged to involve family members spanning all generations in class projects. The result is a partnership of teacher, student, and family in which everyone is learning. Through the involvement of the child's entire family in the various celebrations and activities, the classroom becomes an extension of the family.

The success of the method is mirrored in the atmosphere of the classroom: Much joy and excitement go into creative writing, research, art, musical compositions, and overall academic studies. These feelings are apparent in committee meetings where children plan and prepare for a celebration, feast, class fair, field trip, or social action project. Teachers in subsequent grades report that the children are creative, responsible, industrious, enthusiastic, curious, cooperative, and skillful; most of them work well independently and approach their highest potential.

That this teaching method has been successful in academic terms is validated by academic testing. In morality judgment interviews, based on the theory of Lawrence Kohlberg, my students' progress was impressive. The interviews are based on logical thinking and not on expected answers. Children are tested on their ability to build concepts of morality through logical thinking. On a scale of 1 to 6, where 6 represents the level attained by Martin Luther King, the scores of these elementary schoolchildren, which were started practically at the bottom of the scale (i.e., 1 and 2 at the outset,) rose by a full point, to 2 and 3, by the end of the project. Students taught with this method show significantly greater improvement in reading and mathematics than other students in the school.

SPECIFIC TEACHING PROJECTS

Five teaching projects are described in *Dream-Makers, Peacemakers, and Heroes*, from conceptualization to creative implementation. Each description is illustrated by work created by the children.

1. The teaching project on *Martin Luther King* (Grades 2 and 5) focused on his role as a man of vision and a peacemaker. Devoted to the concept of justice, he was guided by strong inner convictions. His strength lay in dealing nonviolently with hard social realities. The objective of the project was to teach children to understand justice through their own experiences and observations. They were encouraged to follow and persevere in their dreams, combining their skills and imagination. The children worked on injustices of people against people and people against nature. Their reconciliation skills were developed by imagining what Martin Luther King might have done in conflicts that arose in class. The children created approximately thirty original approaches to conflict resolution, which included using comedy, role-playing, and puppetry as techniques. Eventually they evolved their own code of peacemaking. They were then encouraged to extend their dreams to include other people's welfare, the state of the world, and the world of nature. Learning how to deal with the subject of death — of animals, family members, friends, or famous personalities — was included in this project. For their social action program, the children "adopted" the senior citizens at the Fort Tryon Nursing Home.

2. The project using *Johnny Appleseed* (Grade 4) as a model focused on ecology, geography, and American history. Johnny Appleseed was a naturalist, a visionary, and a peacemaker between American Indians and settlers. In the 1790s he walked from Massachusetts to Illinois planting apple seeds. His only possessions were a huge bag filled with apple seeds, a Bible, and a tin pot that he used alternatively as a hat and as a cooking vessel. He was a trailblazer, making his way across the country through harsh conditions. Among others, Johnny Appleseed influenced the life of Abraham Lincoln. In this project the children followed Johnny's footsteps from East Coast to the Midwest, learning geography and history as they retraced his route.

Johnny Appleseed was also America's first conservationist. To understand this role, the children worked with various environmental centers in the New York City area, with Friends of the Hopi Indians, and with Pete Seeger's sloop, *Clearwater*, which seeks to reestablish the Hudson River as a pollutant-free waterway. The children raised funds for the Clearwater Sloop project, planted gardens in the classrooms, and built bird feeders to raise funds for their celebrations.

3. The story of the *Iroquois Great Tree of Peace* (Grade 3) served as another teaching model. The Iroquois believe that all weapons of war were buried under a white pine tree. Its roots reached into the four directions of the earth. A peacemaker went to all warring tribes and united them. Inspired by this symbol of peace, the children incorporated their own images of peace in stories, poetry, music, and art. This project emphasized learning about gratitude, respect, the interdependence of all life, communication (picture-writing, sign language, language of animals, plants, and birds), and stereotyping and prejudice. The children were also encouraged to learn the value of silence as a way of listening to the natural world, to others, and to their own inner thoughts. Indian legends were used to help the children get in touch with the apparently simple yet extraordinary miracles around them. The identification of miracles in our daily lives was a recurring theme and, as the year progressed, the children became increasingly sensitive to and appreciative of the world surrounding them. The Indian clan system was studied as a model for the extended family in the classroom. For social action projects the children worked with the Akwesasane Mohawk Freedom School and the Fieldston School.

4. The children of Grade 5 created the Patchworkers project as their original concept of peace. Through the study and creation of patchwork quilts, they learned in depth about designs, patterns, shapes, and forms in nature and art. The theme of the Patchworkers stressed that if all the children combined the very best of their talents, skills, ideas, and resources in a cooperative and generous way, they would then be able to create something useful, beautiful, and harmonious. The project formed the Patchworker Rescue Service, which aimed to patch up disputes between children in the school and between the children and the administration. Various reconciliation techniques were developed in the Patchworkers Traveling Puppet Theater, in cartoons, jokebooks, improvisation, mime, and skits. During the year the children divided into various Patchworker groups consisting of musicians, singers, playwrights, actors, and storytellers, demonstrating how peer teaching, skill sharing, and a talents exchange service could be the process leading to a unifying force in the classroom. Their social action program consisted of distributing handmade quilts and performing for local nursing homes.

5. Dancing Colors and Singing Buildings was created by children from four kindergarten classes, two regular and two bilingual. It revolves around the beauty and joy found in the movement of colors and sounds. Many stories, games, songs, poems, plays, dances, and murals were created around this theme. Some depicted conflicts; others showed how to live in harmony. The children were divided into several groups of colors and sounds. They formed their own kindergarten apprenticeship system of colorists, designers, composers, conductors, and rhythm makers. They discovered how to create new colors and sounds, and as they mastered their new skills, they moved on to the next color and sound group. This project encouraged the children to explore the harmonies that exist with colors and sounds as well as to celebrate their differences. Five children from each class were chosen to form the Kindergarten Art Club. These children provided art shows for the community. Three of the winners of the statewide "I Love New York" contest and the winner of first prize in the Women's History Month contest were selected from this Kindergarten Art Club.

First Things: Imagination and Assumptions

The selection that follows, like the first selection, was chosen because it models two essential elements of effective and responsible peace education, the pedagogical goal of releasing and nurturing the powers of the imagination, and the professional obligation to articulate the basic assumptions underlying this goal. Early childhood educator Sherrill Akyol has successfully integrated these elements into her curriculum, "Deliberate Peace Education."

Meditation and prayer are widely advocated as spiritual approaches to peace, but their developmental and educational possibilities have been given only limited consideration. We believe them to be especially promising means for the development of imagination as a cognitive skill. Teachers who come to peace education out of an initial concern with classroom conflict and discipline may also find this exercise a useful way to achieve positive behavioral changes.

The acknowledgment of intentionality and the stipulation of value assumptions are other exemplary characteristics of Ms. Akyol's entry. The curriculum reveals her working assumptions about peace (widely shared by peace educators) and provides mechanisms for pursuing the learning objectives she has derived from her assumptions. Among the most important are the need for a broad repertoire of conflict resolution behaviors, the positive cumulative effects of cooperative thinking and behavior, and the need to confront fear. All of these behaviors are assumed as essential to peace.

SELECTION 2
Deliberate Peace Education

Entrant: Sherrill Akyol
School: P.S. 75M, New York, NY 10025
Grade Level: K–6
Concepts: Peace is an experience; practice makes it more possible and able to be generalized.
Topics: Exercises for personal peace practices.
Instructional Methods: Induction
Cognitive Objectives: Develop an attitude toward conflict based on peace values and skills of peaceful problem solving.
Affective Objectives: Holding the belief that peace is possible; it begins with the individual.

INTRODUCTION

"Nuclear peace education," as it is generally conceived, seeks to explore the costs of the nuclear arms race. It focuses on the various arguments used to support the arms build-up and the various fears that each side of the race projects onto the other. "Deliberate peace education," however, is appropriate for any set of circumstances where conflict is an issue. Its goals are to broaden our students' understanding of conflict and to help them develop creative strategies for resolving it.

When students are first asked to think about peace, they report images of flowers, quiet or happy songs, still lakes and outdoor scenery, and good physical feelings. Often it appears that they find many of these images boring. It's as if only so much "peace" is tolerable.

It is important for educators to help students broaden their images of peace so that it is seen not so much as the absence of conflict, but as constructive nonviolent conflict that helps to foster growth on a variety of levels (personal, organizational, community, global). Conflict is best understood as a characteristic of a healthy organism. It should not be confused with our often inadequate response to it. Deliberate peace education aims to develop our students' skills for resolving interpersonal conflict.

ASSUMPTIONS UNDERLYING DELIBERATE PEACE EDUCATION

1. Violence is not a solution, but a consequence to be avoided. People are not for hitting.

2. The best solution is one where both sides win. If there is a winner and a loser, both have lost.

3. There is always enough to go around. Competition is a form of aggression that manifests itself in win-lose activities.

4. There is a more positive/peaceful form for thinking/believing that takes practical effect (as in *The 100th Monkey* by Ken Keyes). Deliberate peace work holds this form in focus, thereby contributing to the "critical mass" buildup of peaceful ways of solving conflict. Contributing to the critical mass increases the chances that these peaceful solutions enter the dominant cultural patterns.

5. Today's children are their parents' teachers, especially in their capacity to be sensitized to peace concerns.

6. Developing a sense of competence is integral to a healthy existence. If children are to become competent, we must allow them to experiment with solutions to their problems. This does not negate the need for guidance, but it asserts that practice is necessary in the development of flexible problem-solving strategies.

PERSONAL PEACE PRACTICE

Show the class pictures of a student losing a typical conflict. Magazines can provide suitable examples. Discuss how students would feel in the situation and how typical the scene is. Use this opportunity to establish that you don't have to talk about something if you don't want to; silence is OK, and we don't talk about what someone else says outside of our classroom. Only our own situation is for us to talk about.

Then brainstorm alternative solutions (N.B.: brainstorming involves no evaluation; it only lists as many possibilities as the class can muster). Pick a few to discuss and ask each person to silently identify a conflict in his or her own life (home or school) and imagine another way of handling it (not previously thought of or tried before).

As an ongoing homework assignment during every day for the next week (7 days), the students are to be aware of one conflict and are to attempt to handle it in a new way. Whether they are successful or not, they are to pay attention to their feelings. They may wish to write them in a diary or *Peace Book*. It is also important to give the students regular opportunities to talk about what they are thinking and learning. To broaden the students' thinking without being judgmental, ask questions about the solutions you consider less desirable.

The following week assign two conflicts per day as homework. New solutions should be tried with parents, siblings, teachers, peers, etc.

Continually stress to the class that every time they exercise a deliberate peace act they are increasing the "critical mass" of peace making—which will contribute to solving the world's problems better. They are also illustrating behaviors that will serve as examples for their parents and elders, thus qualifying themselves as teachers.

TALK-IT-OVER CHAIRS

Two disputants are each given a chair that is confined to a small assigned area (a corner, rug, area by a bookshelf or teacher's desk, etc.); they are told that they may turn the chair any way they want in that space, but their task is to resolve the problem in a mutually acceptable way. It is important that the teacher not intervene while the children are engaged in the process, but be ready with praise and acceptance once they have reached accord. Principals and others who find themselves continuously mediating interpersonal disputes or giving negative attention will find this very useful.

"WHEN AFRAID" LIST

These various suggestions (from L. Mercado, Principal, *Community Principal's Newsletter*, no. 6 [22 Nov. 1983], P.S. 75M, 735 West End Ave., New York, NY 10025) have been made by and tested by grade schoolers (Grades 1–6). The list may be lengthened by students at your school; it serves best as a menu that reminds the student of possibilities.

1. Do something good for someone else.
2. Do something to move around (bike, jump, run, football, etc.).
3. Imagine yourself or pretend to be in a favorite place.
4. Get hugs.
5. Draw pictures to get it out of your mind.
6. Talk about how you feel.
7. For bad dreams: put light on
                     hug teddy bear, person, favorite animal
                     walk around
                     fall asleep with someone you like
                     sing a little song.

RELAXATION WORK

Lying and sitting still and concentrating on a steady sound, or just the breath, allows a passive consciousness to develop. Practicing this technique 15–20 minutes daily as a group will lead to a lifetime skill in taking charge of one's own "cooling out." Classroom practice allows the teacher to:

1. Call for 5 minutes of silence during a heated period.
2. Prepare for an intense period of work (such as tests) or creativity.
3. Use the state for guided imagery to explore the individual's oneness with the planet, other humans, new solutions to old problems.

An example of a guided imagery.   Sit back, with both feet flat. Let your hands be comfortable, and close your eyes. If some of you are more comfortable with your heads on the desk, O.K. Concentrate on your breathing; notice how it just happens; you don't force it. Your breath breathes you . . . (2 min.). Now let yourself feel your skin as it touches the air just around your body; feel your energy flowing into the space . . . (2 min.). You can't tell where your breathing energy stops and the rest of the room's space starts. Notice that your breathing is very slow . . . and your physical body feels quite heavy but light at the same time. . . . Now let your breathing reach to the walls and feel how extended you are (2 min.). Let your breath energy go down the hall and be around our school building. . . . Notice how quiet your body is but how fast your energy travels (2 min.). Find someone who needs your help, and let your energy be there (3 min.). Now grow your breathing even farther into the street and see your energy changing to kindness and peace there (3 min.). Enter the nearest tree, and feel its energy . . . (3 min.). Now, very gently, become aware of your breathing and yourself right here in our room, and slowly open your eyes and come back at your own pace.

Lights back on; talk about it, if a student wishes. This is an early experience. After it is established practice, you can have silent, other-led, or taped meditation time.

Students can learn to call for 3–5 minutes of silence as an active technique when conducting meetings, preparing for games, etc.

Studying Cultures: Respecting and Appreciating Others

It is important to remember that human beings are usually persuaded to fight wars against "enemies," and enemies are always different, the difference being perceived as negative, or evil. Enemy images are born in these negative notions of others, nurtured by stereotypes that reduce others to a few negative characteristics, and fortified by prejudices that deny the others their full humanity (Reardon, 1985). These images, stereotypes, and prejudices are easily manipulated because they are so simple. Those who hold and believe them can be denied their full rights of reflection and decision making on questions of national security and the waging of war. And they are readily persuaded to deny virtually all rights to the "enemy," including and especially the right to live. Preventing and transcending these negative notions about people of different cultures, races, classes, or ideologies is a major task for peace education, especially when it is conceived in terms of negative peace, the prevention of war.

When peace education is set in terms of positive peace, education to provide knowledge, understanding, and appreciation of other cultures can become the basis for both improved human relations and a richer quality of life. By viewing human differences as interesting and enriching, we broaden our range of possible experiences and expand the pool of human potential from which we can derive possibilities for the resolution of our common global problems. We thus take a step toward developing a world view that encompasses all of humanity, enjoys diversity, and cherishes all human life.

We see in the curriculum submitted by Susan Hopkins of the Children's Center of California State University at Fullerton the tools for providing young children with early cross-cultural education as the basis for this essential aspect of education for positive peace. The suggestions here will provide an opportunity for young children to learn about differences and similarities between American and Asian cultures while introducing them to everyday aspects of Asian life, food, art, clothes, and language. These techniques could be adapted to teaching about various other cultures of the world.

SELECTION 3
Asian Culture Curriculum

Entrant: Susan D. Hopkins
School: Children's Center, California State University, Fullerton, 800 N. State College Blvd., Fullerton, CA 92634
Grade Level: Kindergarten and Pre-kindergarten
Subject: Integrated curriculum — all subject areas integrated within theme.
Concepts: People everywhere in the world have the same basic needs for food, clothing, shelter, communication, recreation, and expressing feelings. However, different cultures have created different ways of meeting

these needs. By studying other cultures we can learn to respect and appreciate the differences and similarities.

Topics: Asian foods, crafts, stories, music, ceremonies, and games.

Instructional Methods: Teachers introduce concepts and activities for children to explore and discover.

Cognitive Objectives: Children will learn

to participate in some customs and traditions from another culture;

to be able to talk about one aspect (craft, food, clothes, holiday) of Asian culture;

to practice fine muscle coordination by doing craft projects;

to experience first-hand a food from an Asian culture.

Affective Objectives: Children will learn

to understand and appreciate people from other cultures;

to develop awareness that it is acceptable to be different;

to become aware that all people have feelings of happiness, pride, sadness, anger, etc.;

to develop friendships with people of other cultures.

CURRICULUM IDEAS

A. Craft Activities

1. Origami — Japanese paper folding.

2. Chinese Dragon made from cartons and boxes — paint boxes, connect with string, and let the children wear the boxes on their heads for a parade. Careful adult supervision is needed as the children can't see through the boxes.

3. Blow Paintings — using straws, tempera paint, and paper. Dip straw into paint, let a drop of paint fall onto paper, then blow through the straw to push paint in wiffly lines. Printing with sponges on other materials can add another dimension to the artwork.

4. Fish Kites — materials needed include wrapping paper, pipe cleaners, glue, and string.

5. Oriental Lanterns — on one day paint the lanterns using soft colors of water color paints. The next day cut the lanterns on the lines indicated on the pattern and staple together. Add a handle. These can be hung up around the room to add to the feeling of Oriental culture.

6. Crepe Paper Prints of Fish — cut fish shape from brightly colored crepe paper. Place cut out fish on manilla paper or newsprint and paint it with vinegar water ($\frac{1}{2}$ vinegar, $\frac{1}{2}$ water). When the paper is dry, peel off the crepe paper fish and see the print underneath.

B. Cooking

1. Tea Eggs — boil one egg per child for 10 minutes. Cool in water. Crack

the shell with a spoon. Combine 3 tablespoons of black tea, 2 table-spoons of salt, and 2 tablespoons of soy sauce and add to the water. Boil eggs in the tea mixture for 20 minutes. Remove shells to discover a pretty pattern.

2. Sushi—use Japanese molds or form into balls with hands.
   Boil together:

   $1/4$ cup sugar

   1 teaspoon MSG

   $1/3$ cup vinegar

   $2^1/_2$ teaspoons salt

   Combine with:

   2 cups cooked rice

   1 cup grated carrot

   Japanese children eat these for their lunches.

3. Egg Foo Yung—grow your own mung beans (see below) and then use them in this dish. Each child cracks one egg into bowl and beats it. Add a small amount each of tuna, shrimp, chopped celery, bean sprouts, and chopped green onion, then stir. Pour into frying pan and fry as a pancake. Season with soy sauce and eat.

C. Science
   1. Grow Mung Beans—children grow their own in baby food jars by covering several seeds with warm water and soaking overnight in a dark place. Then drain and rinse at least twice daily for 4 or 5 days. When sprouted they are ready to use in Egg Foo Yung.
   2. Silkworms—silkworm eggs can often be gotten from school districts or local colleges. They hatch when mulberry trees leaf out and then must feed on the mulberry leaves constantly until they spin their cocoons. The children take much interest in feeding them, watching them grow and change. Charts showing changes can be developed with the children.
   3. Carp Fish—using photographs of fish help the children compare the looks and uses of carp and other kinds of fish. Charts of comparisons may be developed.

D. Stories
   1. Flack, Marjorie. *The Story About Ping*, (New York: Viking Press, 1933).
   2. Matsuno, Masako. *A Pair of Red Clogs* (New York: Putnam, 1981).
   3. Mosel, Arlene. *The Funny Little Woman* (New York: Dutton, 1977).
   4. Mosel, Arlene. *Tikki Tikki Tembo* (New York: Scholastic Book Services, 1968).
   5. Wyndham, Robert. *Chinese Mother Goose Rhymes*, (New York: World Publishing, 1968).

E. Dramatics
  1. Using clothes from various Asian countries, try them on, compare how they look and feel, and use them in role playing how families live in Asia.
  2. Lower tables (remove legs if necessary) so that children sit on mats on the floor to eat their meals.
  3. Use chopsticks for eating.
  4. Japanese Tea Ceremony — all remove shoes and sit on the floor for the ceremony.
F. Movement Exploration and Music
  1. Dragon walk — move like a dragon. Create different ways of moving.
  2. Using Ann Barlin's "Shojojo" song from multicultural record for moving like a badger.
  3. Any music from Asian culture can be listened to as background music. Children may also enjoy simply moving to it and/or playing rhythm instruments along with it.
  4. Scarves can be used by children as they move to music.
G. Language
  1. Learning a few words in another language is fun for the children and helps them relate to a different culture.
  2. Discussion of major cultural concepts, with much opportunity for the children to express their thoughts, is important.
  3. Language Experience stories can be created about the various activities in the classroom.
H. Special Events: It is very important to include any families of Asian background in the unit of study. These families can contribute ideas and materials and bring a richness to the unit in very special ways. And, of course, their children feel great pride in their heritage. Do invite them to contribute.

Concepts for Peace: Community Responsibility

"Project Peace," submitted by the James Conger Elementary School, is the work of a team of teachers that included Judith A. Dunham, Juliann S. Secrest, Lois K. Smith, Rhonda L. Tyree, and Sally A. Wetmore. While it is designated for kindergarten through fifth grade, it might best be used for children in grades three and four. Youngsters of this age are just beginning to develop a sense of order and still need the help of adult judgment in some decision making. It is also an age when respect for others and for self is an important aspect of positive socialization, and when learning to attend to others becomes the basis for observing rights and for the cultivation of wider learning possibilities.

Particularly notable in this curriculum is its emphasis on peace as something to be constructed. Peace results from specific behaviors and is maintained by particular skills. Noteworthy among them are skills of communication, most especially active listening, a complement to the notion of nonjudgmental listening.

At the core of this curriculum is a recognition of the importance of fulfilling the emotional and physical needs of children as a prerequisite to all learning, particularly learning to be peacemakers. Self-actualization and the development of a strong sense of social competency and personal capacities are a major emphasis of this curriculum. We believe these to be essential elements for early childhood peace education.

Social responsibility as the indicator of social competence is also a significant element to be stressed. Teaching children to care for others is a first step in teaching them to be socially responsible.

SELECTION 4
Project Peace

Entrant: Project Peace Team
School: James Conger Elementary School, Channing St., Delaware, OH
    43015
Grade Level: K–5
Subject: Various
Concepts:
    Definition of Peace
    Peace Promotion
    Peacekeeping
    Peace Publicity
Topics: The unit focuses on peace at a personal level spiraling to the global
    community.
Materials: See bibliography
Instructional Methods:
    Brainstorming
    Role playing
    Singing
    Writing
    Group or individual discussions

Reading
Research
Cognitive Objectives: Defining peace, conflict, and fighting.
Affective Objectives: Developing and applying strong communication,
    interaction, and decision-making skills advancing the promotion of
    peace. Additionally, peacekeeping techniques are integrated into the
    children's lives, as is the commitment to publicizing peace.

INTRODUCTION

It is better to light just one little candle,
    than to stumble in the dark;
Better far that you light just one little candle,
    all you need's a tiny spark

In his theory of growth motivation, Abraham H. Maslow, the founder
of humanistic psychology, views need gratification as the foundation to all
human development [*Toward a Psychology of Being* (Princeton, NJ: Van
Nostrand, 1968)]. Maslow assumes that all children possess a natural
positive striving towards self-growth. One can only realize one's potential
development when one's needs are met. Maslow orders these needs as
physiological, safety, love and belonging, esteem, self-actualization, desire
to know and understand, and aesthetic needs. Because it is "safe" to cling to
the lower levels of the development hierarchy, it is imperative that educators
help children meet these basic needs so they may progress toward the higher
levels.

In this unit, Maslow's theory of growth motivation is applied to peace
education. Peace is equated to self-actualization. Self-actualization is
defined here as the functioning of all of one's facilities, the utilization of
one's self-concept and skills. It is this level that the unit focuses on.

Achieving self-actualization is symbolically viewed as lighting one's
candle. Before the candle can be ignited educators must be sure the child
stands firmly on a strong foundation. The foundation, or candlestick, is
constituted of Maslow's four basic needs. The child must be healthy, feel
secure, feel loved, and have a sense of self-worth in order to shine his/her
peace.

And if everyone lit just one little candle,
What a bright world this would be.

INTERACTION SKILLS

Interaction skills have a strong impact on promoting peace. Being considerate, obeying rules, caring actively, being open to active caring, and sharing one's self all work to promote peace.

Being considerate means being polite and respectful of the rights of others. One aspect of respecting the rights of others is being able to abide by rules and guidelines.

Active caring implies extra effort toward strengthening relationships by helping others, giving compliments and other "positive strokes," taking time to show real interest in others, and showing kindness. At the receptive end of active caring, one must be open to those efforts to further the advancement of a peaceful relationship.

Being considerate and caring actively provide an atmosphere of mutual trust that allows people to freely share thoughts, feelings, and intimacies. It is important that both parties share themselves to tighten the peace bond.

PEACEKEEPING PROCEDURE

Even with peace promotion techniques, conflict will occur. The individual must be prepared with creative and nonviolent conflict resolution options. As conflicts arise individuals can practice the following model to keep the peace:

Peacekeeping Model

1. Step back
   a. Take a deep breath
   b. Collect thoughts, feelings, facts
2. Share
   a. Take turns talking clearly and actively listening
   b. Clarify by repeating what you think you hear
3. Solve
   a. Consider options
   b. Choose and act
4. Move forward

Peacekeeping Techniques

Using words to solve problems
Applying communication, interaction, and decision-making skills
Utilizing a mediator (an unbiased adult or friend, if necessary)

Using "I" statements ("I feel . . ." rather than "You always . . .")
Attacking the problem, not the person ("What you *did* made me angry"
    rather than "*You* made me angry")
Attacking the problem at hand without dragging in past problems

Peacekeeping Activities

Reflect and chart how the mediator guides the actors in "the fight" for
    peace. Present the Peacekeeping Procedure as an effective option
    to resolving everyday conflict. Have small groups creatively drama-
    tize a conflict resolved through the Peacekeeping Procedure. Vid-
    eotape, review, and share with other classes, if applicable.
Have students create Peace Pamphlets outlining the Peacekeeping Pro-
    cedure to distribute to other classes.
Share a short biography of Martin Luther King as a famous peacemak-
    er, emphasizing his preaching of solving problems with words.
    Draw upon recent classroom conflicts to test them for use of Dr.
    King's suggestions.
Categorize "I" versus "You" statements written out on sentence strips to
    determine which has a more peaceful effect on the individual (e.g.,
    "I feel angry" vs. "You make me mad").
Exemplify and emphasize the importance of attacking the problem and
    not the person. Have children use person and problem response
    cards (e.g., "You make me so mad!" vs. "Pushing really makes me
    cross").
Set up and discuss drama where one actor offends another who then
    attacks all the offender's faults instead of the particular one at
    hand. Do a second drama attacking the problem and compare the
    two.
Set up a class-versus-teacher conflict in which the children use the
    Peacekeeping Model and Techniques to approach the problem, but
    the teacher clams up. Discuss the need for a Peacekeeper to be
    open and honest as well as how to deal with a closed or noncaring
    person.

COMMUNICATION SKILLS

Communication skills have a strong impact on promoting peace. One
must be able to express oneself clearly and to listen actively. Expression
skills that promote peace include utilization of peace vocabulary, adeptness
at complimenting and being positive, effective utilization of one's voice and
tone quality, and appropriate choice of discrete words and phrases in in-

teracting with others. An additional expression skill is the ability to share one's feelings both verbally and nonverbally. Active listening skills are contained in the following model:

1. Be attentive
2. Do not interrupt
3. Hear what is really being said
   a. Listen with your eyes
   b. Listen for tone
   c. Listen for feelings
4. Consider (and, if necessary, clarify) what is being said
5. React

BIBLIOGRAPHY

Books

Lionni, Leo. (1968). *The alphabet tree*. New York: Pantheon.
Steiner, Claude. (1977). *Warm fuzzy tale*. Sacramento: Julmar Press.
Viorst, Judith. (1972). *Alexander and the terrible, horrible, no good, very bad day*. New York: Atheneum.
Zolotow, Charlotte. (1963). *The quarreling book*. New York: Harper & Row.

Songs

Kaiser, Kurt. (1969). "Pass It On." Newbury Park, CA: Lexicon Press.
Miller, Sy, & Jill Jackson. (1955). "Let There Be Peace on Earth." Delaware Water Gap, PA: Shawnee Press.
Mysels, George, & J. Maloy Roach. (1951). "Light One Little Candle." Delaware Water Gap, PA: Shawnee Press.
Sherman, Richard M., & Robert B. Sherman. (1963). "It's a Small World." Burbank, CA: Wonderland Press.
Wayman, Joe, & Don Mitchell. (1975). "I Have Feelings." In Gary Grimm & Don Mitchell (Eds.), *Dandylions never roar book*. Carthage, IL: Good Apple.

SECTION II
The Elementary Grades (4–6)

Awareness of Cultural Diversity and Universal Human Dignity

As children move toward a more developed sense of personal and group identity, their knowledge of differences and their attitudes toward them become more important to their growing capacities to become peacemakers. It is absolutely essential that the fundamental notion of universal human dignity be the center from which children learn to relate to each other. As they begin to encounter public issues and social problems and to learn problem-solving techniques, they should be guided in their approach to such matters by a set of criteria that make the preservation and enhancement of human dignity a necessary outcome of any proposed personal action or public policy. Human dignity is the core of the concept of positive human relationships and the ultimate indicator of a just global society (see Selection 7). In current peace education, it is seen as one of the three fundamentals essential to a comprehensive program: relationship, citizenship, and stewardship.

Relating these concepts to learning about the larger society beyond the classroom can be undertaken at Grades 4 through 6 (ages 9–11). At this stage children are likely to have greater understanding of human differences (and, it is to be hoped, some experience with such differences) and an awareness of a world in which human fulfillment is impeded by problems resulting from human behavior. It is important for peace education to stress the origins of such problems in terms of knowledge, choices, and alternative possibilities. Youngsters can begin to learn about how the world is in the context of how it might be (Greene, 1985). As children learn of the problems resulting from conflict, ignorance, poor choice making, and lack of imagination, they should simultaneously learn of the possibilities of imagining and working for solutions to many of these problems (see Selection 5). They need as well to conceive of and practice specific actions and behaviors that they themselves can undertake, such as the resolution of their own conflicts (see Selection 9).

23

Creative Imagination and Problem Solving

At this stage, there also needs to be an emphasis on the potential that learning and knowledge offer to the solution of human problems. Children can be helped to understand that what they learn in their study of literature (see Selection 6), language arts, science, or any subject can help them to contribute to the society as well as to reach their personal goals. Social responsibility should be one of the first concepts learned in a comprehensive peace education program. Problem-solving skills are basic to carrying out social responsibility, as is an attitude of hopefulness in the face of problems.

Two fundamental notions integral to peace education—that peace is problematic and that life is to be celebrated—need to be communicated at this stage (see Selection 8). Equally fundamental, and especially important to elementary social education, is the idea that people can, and frequently do, change society and resolve very grave, overwhelming social problems.

The problem-solving approach is one way to deal with children's fears of nuclear war, which are often similar to adult "worries" about war, violence, and injustice (see Selection 8). Teachers might also consider organizing for themselves a workshop on responses to nuclear fears, forming a support group of colleagues or parents and teachers to deal with these concerns, or at the very least familiarizing themselves with the work of Joanna Rogers Macy (1983) on this topic.

A problem focus provides topics through which to weave the conceptual threads of justice and development throughout the curriculum at all grade levels and in all subjects. A global problem such as hunger is suited to infusion (see, for example, Selection 30) but also lends itself to discrete units (see Selection 10) undertaken by individual teachers. This particular topic, for example, not only provides the basis for studying problems of global development, economic injustice, and structural violence, but offers excellent possibilities for skills development, especially in the life sciences, social studies, and mathematics, and is an excellent subject for a generalized problem-solving approach (Jacobson, 1982).

Empowerment is a goal to be sought through the development of creative capacities and imagination. Imagination can produce various creative processes—from the free-form brainstorming proposed by Monson (Selection 5) to the more disciplined "imaging" of specific conditions and circumstances that the Haipt-Cooke curriculum (Selection 6) calls for—and has a role to play in all subjects and at all grade levels of peace education. When applied in the higher grades to the problem of the institutional requirements of peacemaking, creative imagination becomes "model building" (see, for example, Selection 21). Peace education seeks to emphasize the cognitive significance of creative imagination and to promote its intentional nurturance in every area and at every level of education. The unprecedented nature and dimensions of the problems of violence and war in our present world call for deliberate development of the capacities of the imagination and the skills of invention and design. These are capacities and skills that must be exercised from the earliest possible stages of the learning process, and further developed at each successive stage.

The following curriculum extracts are designed to develop these concepts of human dignity and social responsibility in the childhood years, while developing imaginative, problem solving, and conflict resolution skills.

Envisioning Alternatives: Imagining a "Perfect World"

Thinking about how the world might be and envisioning a society characterized by justice are the essence of conceptualizing the conditions that comprise positive peace. If we are to educate for peace, both teachers and students need to have some notion of the transformed world we are educating for. The capacity to imagine a transformed society, to describe to ourselves and others what a better, more humane global order might be like is essential to peacemaking. We must keep the development of this capacity paramount among our learning objectives. For this reason we begin this second section of elementary level curricula as we did the first, with exercises to develop imaginative skills. The following excerpt is also an example of material suitable to "transition" grades that span two developmental stages as they are delimited in the sequence proposed here for a comprehensive peace education program; this particular excerpt spans the early childhood and upper elementary grades.

Speculating about and practicing change in our own realities is perhaps the most effective education for political and social efficacy. Many peace educators believe such experience is essential to developing the sense of empowerment needed for responsible pro-active world citizenship.

The curriculum of Jill Monson demonstrates one specific activity designed to achieve such objectives in third- through fifth-grade classes. Teachers undertaking to pursue Monson's objectives might introduce this unit into a study of global problems and human conflict. As they work with the study of conflict, teachers also need to attend carefully to the issue of "nonjudgmental listening." Educators at all levels—from early childhood through graduate school—must strive to help learners to develop this capacity.

SELECTION 5
How I Might Improve the World

Entrant: Jill Monson
School: Wildwood Park Elementary School, 2601 Wildwood Park Drive,
   Puyallup, WA 98374
Grade Level: Third through Fifth Grades
Subject Area: Guidance
Concepts: Global cooperation, stewardship of the Earth, racial and social
   justice.
Topics: Nuclear arms race, civil rights, pollution, hunger.
Materials: Filmstrip and cassette ("The Best of All Possible Worlds," from
   Argus Communications, Niles, IL), paper, pencils.
Instructional Methods:
   1) Presentation of a/v material
   2) Class discussions from open-ended questions
   3) Assignment of in-class paper/pencil activity
Cognitive Objectives:
   1) Learning that *many* elements affect the quality of life and that each
      of us can have an impact on those elements
   2) Heightened global awareness and understanding of individual re-
      sponsibility to the world community
Affective Objectives:
   1) Increased feeling of responsibility for how *I* affect my world
   2) Development of capacity for nonjudgmental listening.

PROCEDURE

1. *Brainstorming Activity:* Ask class: "If you were to offer *one* idea for
a more perfect world, what would it be?" (List *all* ideas on the board, with
no discussion or judgment.) Once all ideas are listed, call for comments on
any of the ideas. Guide the comments to be made in an objective, non-put-
down manner.

2. *Show filmstrip* "The Best of All Possible Worlds" (Argus Communication, Niles, IL). This 96-frame sound filmstrip "is a story of a kind and
fair god who was determined to create a world completely free of pain and
misery. Discussion should encourage open feelings and reactions to a personal identification with a 'perfect world'" (from the Operation Manual and
Discussion Guide).

Ask: "Were any of our ideas included in the filmstrip story?" Discuss.

3. *Each student does a paper* entitled, "My ideas for a Perfect World"
(written and/or pictorial). Discuss these ideas and direct the discussion to:

"What could *you* do to make the world more perfect?" (e.g., get along with the person at the next desk, get along better with my brothers and sisters, solve playground problems without hitting, clean up around my neighborhood, re-cycle, make sure I never abuse narcotics, etc.)

4. *Keep/display papers.* Refer to them later: "How do you think you're doing with your ideas about making the world more perfect?"

Concepts of Peace:
The Use of Imaging and Children's Literature

Mildred Haipt and Jane Cooke provide some very useful theoretical background and a sound developmental rationale for the use of imaging and sensory learning experience. While other curricula offer more specific instructional procedures, Haipt and Cooke provide a concise, integrating framework and an excellent bibliography as essential background to such procedures. All peace educators intending to undertake imaging and creative approaches to peace education in the elementary grades are urged to familiarize themselves with the material in their bibliography.

Since it is essential that the capacity to elicit and nurture these skills be developed in teachers and the development of this specific competency is a task of teacher education, the Haipt-Cooke curriculum was also designed for use in university level courses in teacher education. Haipt and Cooke have further developed these ideas in their monograph, *Thinking with the Whole Brain: An Integrative Teaching/Learning Model* (Washington, DC: National Education Association, 1986).

SELECTION 6
Developing Concepts of Peace Through Children's Literature

Entrant: Mildred Haipt and Jane Cooke

School: Education Department, College of New Rochelle, School of Arts and Sciences, 29 Castle Place, New Rochelle, NY 10801

Grade Level: Primary grades and college students in teacher preparation.

Subject: Reading/Language Arts

Concepts: Cooperation, Communication, Friendship, Compassion, Non-violence, Multi-cultural Understanding

Topics: 6 storybooks: *Swimmy, Frog and Toad Together, Sadako and the Thousand Paper Cranes, The Stranger, The Terrible Thing That Hap-*

pened at Our House, and *The Story of Ferdinand* [see Bibliography at the end of this selection]

Materials: Books noted above and simple art materials such as: drawing paper, construction paper, poster paint, bristle-type brushes, cellulose sponges, water bowls, paste, scissors, pasteable materials, and old magazines.

Instructional Methods:

Teacher reads story and children listen attentively.

Teacher guides students through an imagery exercise.

Students draw/paint or make a three-dimensional art work that represents their thoughts and feelings about the values expressed in the story.

Students describe in words what they have produced visually.

Cognitive Objectives: To enable the students to understand abstract concepts (such as cooperation, communication, friendship) that are otherwise difficult to explain or define in a way meaningful to children. The model employs stories selected from contemporary realistic fiction and art forms to arrive at this understanding. The children's descriptions of their art products will indicate their understanding of the concept.

Affective Objectives:

a. To stimulate imagination so students will identify with characters and plot of stories, thereby coming to understand and appreciate the values portrayed.

b. To provide opportunities through art to explore feelings and ideas engendered by stories and imaging exercises.

INTRODUCTION / RATIONALE

The model, contained in this unit, is based upon Jerre Levy's (1983) synthesis of research on the right and left sides of the brain. In summarizing the research to date, Levy stresses "interhemispheric integration" as a key to understanding the brain and how it functions. He concludes that in the normal person "both hemispheres contribute important and critical processing operations. The final level of understanding or output cannot be allocated to one hemisphere or the other" (p. 68). The challenge is to present content of sufficient complexity and richness to engage both sides of the brain and to facilitate an integration of their respective and simultaneous activities (p. 70).

Secondly, the model affirms the relationship between the imagination and the work of the intellect. Harry S. Broudy (1979), a prominent educational philosopher, points out that our minds are being stocked with images and associations with words and things from the moment of our birth. Everything that impinges on our senses—visual, auditory, tactile, kinesthetic, olfactory—becomes part of our "image-conceptual store" (p. 348). Whenever we read, speak, write, or listen to speech, images and associations are activated. They enable us to recognize and to understand our experiences. For, just as our knowledge is sensory-dependent, so too is our comprehension and understanding of that knowledge.

The procedure used in the model involves the student in visual as well as verbal thinking. It might be described as a verbal-visual-verbal thinking model. There is a shift from one form of thinking to another so as to provide complementarity and integration of these two important mental processes. The students draw upon both memory—representations of the past or present that come before the mind's eye—and imagination images, pictures that are constructed from various elements of our sensory experiences.

PROCEDURES

1. The students listen to one of the stories listed with attention. The teacher shows the book's illustrations while reading and attempts to focus on the story's theme at appropriate points.

2. The students follow the teacher through an imagery exercise that is related to the theme of the story and to the peace concept(s) contained in it.

Bagley and Hess (1982) recommend that students be introduced to imagery exercises in several steps over a two-week period. The initial exercises invite students to look at objects and then turn away and see them with the mind's eye. Gradually, the students are guided by the teacher to draw on their memories and to invoke a number of their senses—seeing, smelling, touching, tasting, and feeling. In the final steps, the students are asked to use their imaginations and to enter the non-real world of fantasy.

In leading the exercises, teachers are urged to speak "slowly, smoothly, in an effortless manner" (p. 46). Bagley and Hess warn against forcing images. Rather, they say "Let them happen!" (p. 42). Students should be given a choice of doing or not doing the exercise. Creating a nonjudgmental atmosphere in the classroom is most conducive to engaging students and stimulating their imaginations.

3. The students draw/paint or make a three-dimensional art work that represents a *mimetic, expressive,* or *conventional mode* of art expression.

Eisner explains these three modes of treating forms of representation in Chapter 3 of his book *Cognition and Curriculum* (1982). Although one may dominate in a work of art, all three forms are often found together.

In the *mimetic* mode, the artist imitates, within the limitations of a particular medium, some aspect of the world that he experiences.

In the *expressive* mode, the artist goes beyond "surface features" and reveals feelings or qualities represented in a given object or event.

In the *conventional* mode, the artist uses language, symbols, and color to convey his thoughts and feelings.

The art activity should flow naturally out of the imagery exercise. It can take any form—drawing, collage, painting, sculpture—to represent the images developed during the exercise. Students are instructed to represent some of the ideas or feelings that they have from the story or imaging.

4. The students describe (orally or in writing) what they have produced visually.

EVALUATION

The children's description of their illustrations and how they represent a given peace concept will indicate whether they have understood the concept or theme of the story and are able to apply it to meaningful situations. It is expected that the students will express the concepts concretely or symbolically as they imagine them or experience them in their own life space, or will express the feeling(s) that the concepts evoke in them.

BIBLIOGRAPHY

General

Arnheim, Rudolf. (1969). *Visual thinking*. Berkeley, CA: University of California Press.

Bagley, Michael T., & Hess, Karin (1982). *200 ways of using imagery in the classroom*. Woodcliff Lake, NJ: New Dimensions of the 80's Publishers.

Broudy, Harry S. (1979, January). "Arts education: Necessary or just nice?" *Phi Delta Kappan, 60*(5), 347–350.

Eisner, Elliot W. (1982). *Cognition and curriculum: A basis for deciding what to teach*. New York: Longman.

Eisner, Elliot W. (1983, March). "On the relationship of conception to representation." *Art Education, 36*(2), 22–27.

Levy, Jerre. (1983, January). "Research synthesis on right and left hemispheres: We think with both sides of the brain." *Educational Leadership, 40*(4), 66–71.

Children's Storybooks (used in the unit)

Blaine, Marge. (1975). *The terrible thing that happened at our house*. New York: Four Winds Press.
Coerr, Eleanor B. (1975). *Sadako and the thousand paper cranes*. New York: Four Winds Press.
Leaf, Munro. (1936). *The story of Ferdinand*. New York: Viking Press.
Leonni, Leo. (1963). *Swimmy*. New York: Pantheon Books.
Lobel, Arnold. (1972). *Frog and toad together*. New York: Harper and Row.
Ringi, Kjell. (1968). *The stranger*. New York: Random House.

The Value of the Human Person: Core Concept for Positive Peace

The concept of positive peace is currently reflected in peace education curricula in the study of the problems of global social justice and issues related to the violation of human rights. Both of these concerns arise from the value placed on the human person and the concept of human dignity. Whether this value emphasizes the individual or persons in relationship, such as in a family, nation, or ethnic group, the humanity and dignity of the person is the central value concept. The desire to fulfill the potential of the human person—and the expansion of the possibilities for doing so—underlies most of that which we call human "progress" or "civilization." That same fulfillment, which is for many the ultimate reason to struggle for "stable" or negative peace (i.e., the abolition of war), is also the inspiration of notions of "dynamic" or positive peace, the conditions of a truly human society.

As a core value of positive peace, human dignity is a concept that should be central and constant throughout peace education, particularly as a primary learning objective of the childhood stage in the development of peacemakers. The next extract was selected because John Schmitt's philosophy of peace education provides an excellent rationale for this early stress on human dignity. The following excerpt from his handbook expresses much of the philosophic basis for the centrality of this concept to a comprehensive peace education program. Such a program would feature the value of human dignity and a commitment to the universal realization of human rights as essential to the development of effective global citizenship.

SELECTION 7
Toward the Dignity of All—A Handbook to Educate for Peace

Entrant: John A. Schmitt
School: Mount Horeb Middle School, 234 South First Street, Mount Horeb, WI 53572
Grade Level: Upper Elementary (Grades 4–6)
Subject: Interdepartmental
Concepts: Curriculum is based on the concept that peace education is a positive means of working toward the dignity of all individuals. Enhancement of self-concept and improvement of relationships are the two basic concepts with which to begin a peace education curriculum for young people.
Topics: Rationale for peace education, knowledge of self, relating with others.
Instructional Methods: Small-group discussion, brain-storming activities, informal short talks and sharing sessions.
Cognitive Objectives: Information about senses and feelings, knowledge of what peace means, group problem-solving skills.
Affective Objectives: Self-appreciation, communicating feelings, increasing capacity to respond to others in need.

INTRODUCTION

God grant me the courage
    to change the things I can change,
the serenity to accept
    those I cannot change,
and the wisdom
    to know the difference.
Anonymous

This handbook has been written to furnish teachers and other educators with a rationale for peace education. Also provided in this handbook are activities and ideas designed to help provide students with a better understanding of what peace is.

Peace education is a positive means of working toward the dignity of all individuals. I am convinced that one of the major challenges to education today is to create a learning environment that promotes the worth of each person. This handbook on peace education is dedicated to the achievement of that purpose.

Peace education has many dimensions. Peace is often thought of only as the absence of war or violence. This negative concept is not adequate. I believe there is a need to carefully broaden the meaning of peace. Peace must become a way of life, based on a positive attitude and a new way of thinking. This demands that we see all human beings not as isolated or insignificant to our own existence, but rather as persons of worth whose survival requires that all humanity work together. This value placed on each person is the bond that draws us all toward the goal of peace.

Peace education can bring about profound changes. We can instill in children a love and respect for all living things, strengthen their sense of their own value as persons, and provide an understanding of the times in which they live. Education can become the cornerstone of peace. Our children are the hopes and promises of tomorrow. We must make their education in the ways of peace a principal concern.

The initial focus of peace education needs to be the way the students see themselves. As educators, we must be concerned about the important role children's feelings of well-being play in their behavior. Teachers must work to create an environment that will nurture feelings of self-worth in students. Children's success in school depends a great deal upon their feeling of self-worth and their self-concepts. Self-concept is the total of all beliefs we hold about ourselves. It is learned as we interact with people and the world. Since the self-concept is learned, it can be enhanced through positive experiences. These positive experiences must be provided by the school. After the home, the school has the greatest impact on the child's development. By enhancing the way children feel about themselves, we can also bring about positive changes in their relationships with others. If we as educators can improve the feelings of self-worth in our students, we can then progress with them to the idea of valuing the importance of others.

We need to make our students more aware of how to cooperate and interact with others. This belief forms the second focus of this handbook. The capacity for warm, interpersonal relationships is essential to positive personal development. We need to make a structured attempt to help students develop the skills necessary to build caring relationships. When students feel good about other people, we all benefit. It starts the positive chain reaction of bringing people together, people who care about each other, as one means of achieving peace. Our students may never change the world, but they themselves will have changed and benefited. They will see the value in positive interactions and also see that their own lives can make a difference.

All too often, schools ignore children's feelings. We can change this by focusing our attention on human skills that emphasize the well-being of children, helping them to form positive relationships. The emotional development of students must be seen as an important aspect of peace education.

Learning to understand feelings can help students feel better about themselves and their world. Through providing experiences that develop an understanding of feelings, we can educate individuals who are more capable of caring about themselves and other people.

The purpose of this handbook on peace education is to increase the scope of what is considered to be peace education and to advocate a view of education that emphasizes the worth of each individual. We need each other to be fully human, and we need a new life style dedicated to peacemaking as the way to achieve human dignity for all people.

From the experiences outlined in this handbook, students will be able to improve their self-esteem, to grow in the areas of cooperation, trust, communication, feelings, and fairness, and to increase their capacity to respond to others in need. As educators, we have a great responsibility to our youth. The forces in our world and the power we have to destroy require us to act. We must educate students to see the wonder in our world and the need for harmony among people. We all have a vast potential within us that needs to be valued and explored. The activities in this handbook are designed to help students experience their potential.

This handbook emphasizes positive peace because it connotes the endeavor to create a system in which violence is unlikely. The notion of positive peace can strengthen the human spirit. It provides hope for awakening a new stage in human history in which persons are truly valued. The difference between negative and positive peace is analogous to the difference between curing an illness and preventing it. Positive peace stresses a personal commitment to the belief that it is not through military strength, but rather through human understanding that we can achieve a more lasting peace.

Positive peace fosters the belief in the equal worth of all human beings. Society is enriched by the diversity and individual differences humans possess. Our students can be shown how rewarding it is to appreciate the vast array of human differences. By helping children to feel good about themselves and their world we can promote their feelings of inner peace. A collective effort toward this goal can begin to build a foundation for achieving positive peace.

Empowerment and Social Change: Dealing with Children's Fears

The curriculum Barbara Gigler of the Meadow Homes School, Concord, California, uses with her combined third- and fourth-grade class confronts the children's fears about nuclear war in a creative and sensitive way. By also eliciting the children's joys and articulating those things that they celebrate and affirm in life, Ms. Gigler provides a balance of fears and joys. This balance is extremely important in providing youngsters with an opportunity to acknowledge and reflect upon both the positive and negative aspects of the world they perceive. For example, in the following extract, activity number 6 introduces to the students in a simple, straightforward, and "natural" manner the important concept that positive change is always possible, an idea that is essential to providing a hopeful attitude toward the resolution of problems of war and injustice.

Gigler offers assurance and personal respect to her elementary level students by making it clear, as she does in activity 5, that it is acceptable to remain silent at times. We all have a right to personal privacy where we need it. Her respect for the children's privacy and/or her sensitivity to any reluctance or unreadiness to share their thoughts is especially important when dealing with fears that may be both very deep and very personal. While Gigler notes the possibility of arousing objections from parents and administration over the "political" nature of the content of her curriculum, teachers also need to exercise care and discretion over the personal and private nature of what children may share. The privacy of families needs to be respected; but responsibility to respond with follow-up action, if necessary, must also be taken. Distress of various kinds, including child abuse, may well emerge in discussions of children's fears and concerns. Teachers intending to use these activities would be well advised to be aware of and prepared for such possibilities.

Teachers must also be careful in their efforts to distinguish between large and small "worries." It is imperative that the children's own sense of magnitude be respected and that none of their personal concerns be diminished.

SELECTION 8
Ideas for Teaching Peace in the Elementary Schools

Entrant: Barbara Gigler
School: Meadow Homes Elementary School, 1371 Detroit Avenue, Concord, CA 94520
Grade Level: K–6
Subject: Social Studies, English, Art
Concepts: Helping elementary school children understand war and peace.
Topics: Nuclear issues, war, peace, empowerment.
Instructional Methods: Class discussion—intimate, structured atmosphere of "Community (Class) Circle."
Cognitive Objectives: Empowerment activities, analyzing, drawing conclusions.

Affective Objectives: Positive, life-affirming activities and projects.

PROCEDURE AND ACTIVITIES

1. *Introduction:* Read aloud any of Joan Anglund's books on friendship, love, or spring, or Charles Schultz' book *Happiness is a Warm Puppy*.

2. *Short discussion:* Ask the children to complete these sentences: "Peace is . . . " and "Peace is not . . . " Later in the day, have the students relax at their desks, heads down, for about 5 to 10 minutes of teacher-directed relaxation of mind and body. It's a good idea to have soft music (no words) in the background. Say to them, "Find a peaceful place in your mind, then relax there and think of what peace means to you." After several minutes, with their heads still down on their desks, pass out $12'' \times 18''$ sheets of paper and crayons or pencils. Quietly explain that they should write the caption, "Peace is . . . " at the top or bottom of their paper and then illustrate the caption. Give them about 12 minutes to do it.

3. *Sounds of Peace:* Put up large poster board or butcher paper. Label it "Sounds of Peace." List on the paper their various suggestions for sounds of peace, such as:

crickets chirping at night

a friend saying "I like you"

me walking through a forest

Later recite together in parts or chants.

4. *Circles of Peace:* Silent time for students. Ask the questions, "What do you love about life?" "What is near and dear to you on the earth?" Then pass out crayons and sheets of paper on which you have already drawn a 4-inch circle outlined with a bright-colored marker. Tell the children, "Fill up the circle with what you love about life." Give them about 15 minutes to do this — no writing, just crayons.

5. *Discussion:* Little Worries, Medium Worries, Big Worries.

Each child may participate (with the right to pass) each time around — little, medium, and then big worries — with a one-sentence reply on each. Narrow this down to 3 or 4 big worries and put them on the board. Have each child choose one worry and write a story about what they could do to change it. (The three main worries in my Grade 3-4 class were nuclear war, earth pollution, and natural disasters such as earthquakes.)

6. *Follow-up discussion on stories:* About half of the stories in my class were written on nuclear war, so I chose that as the discussion topic. I mentioned they had some good ideas as to what to do about nuclear war and then asked:

"What is nuclear war?"

"What is it that you are afraid of?"

About 5 children chose to participate in this discussion. We sat quiet and reflective for a few moments only. I then asked:

"What ever happened to slavery in the U.S.?"

"Why couldn't your great-grandmothers vote, but your mom can?"

"What ever happened to polio?"

Enough answers were given, followed by a period of silence. Then I asked, "What am I trying to tell you?" Some spoke at once, *"Things can change!"* I asked, "What makes things change?" They answered, *"People."* I said, "You're right!" *Smiles — relief!!*

This discussion can be continued by asking, in an excited tone of voice, "What problem or hard time have you had that you changed?" Give them time to reflect on this — then those who want can share. This leads into next activity.

7. *Empowerment Activity*

    Materials: 6 × 9 pastel construction paper

              crayons/pencil

"Remember — think of a time that you had a problem or hard time and you were able to change it."

Have each child draw a line across the middle of the paper. "On one side of the line draw a picture of the problem. On the other side, illustrate and write a brief explanation of what you did to change it." These may be shared. During sharing time, ask what qualities enabled them to make this change. Discuss these qualitites.

8. *The look of peace — Collage*

    Materials: 3' × 5' or larger poster board

              magazines

              glue

              felt pen

              construction paper

Have children tear out magazine pictures that remind them of PEACE. (These include families, nature, animals, church, children, nursing mother, father and child, skiing, map, space, picture of Earth — can also include words.)

9. *Brainstorming:* This activity should follow various discussions on war and peace. Ask the children, "What can be done about the threat of nuclear war?" Any answer is accepted and written on board or butcher paper. When finished, star and discuss some of the ideas they like best. Recall empowerment activities.

10. *Peacemaker discussion:* Questions asked and discussed:

    "What *is* a peacemaker?"

    "Who is a peacemaker at home?"

    "Who is a peacemaker among your friends? At school?"

"Were *you* a peacemaker anytime this week? How?"
"Is it possible that there is a peacemaker within *each one of us*?"

Conflict: A Community Process

Peace education attempts to develop an understanding that conflict and peace are not mutually exclusive. Indeed, conflict is a constant factor in human life, affecting all levels of human social organization. All communities manifest conflicts. Excessive and destructive conflict, however, can weaken and ultimately destroy a community. The peacefulness of a society is not so much determined by the number of conflicts it sustains as by how it deals with conflict. Fair, nonviolent, easy-to-follow, and universally known procedures for conflict resolution are the cornerstone of a peaceful and democratic society. Development of skills for confronting and resolving conflict and knowledge of various communal procedures for dealing with conflict are essential learning objectives in citizenship education.

The interrelationship between conflict and community is illustrated by the following curriculum by Josephine Brokaw, retired from the Ann Arbor, Michigan, Public Schools. Also included is her cover letter. The specific events she recounts demonstrate the practical possibilities of teaching about conflict resolution as a communal responsibility within the context of the students' actual experience.

Ms. Brokaw indicates that this approach is suitable for any grade level. It seems most appropriate to the childhood stage in Grades 4–6, where it is important that children have practical experience with democratic principles, social responsibility, and conflict resolution. The unit also lends itself very well to cooperative learning (Johnson & Johnson, 1984).

SELECTION 9
Peaceful Resolution of Conflicts

Entrant: Josephine Brokaw
School: Ann Arbor Public School, S. State Road, Ann Arbor, MI 48104
Grade: Any
Department: Social Studies
Concepts: People organize themselves into communities of various kinds. Conflicts often arise due to special needs and interests. Knowledge is needed to resolve these conflicts peaceably.

Topics: Organization of communities (cities, states, countries, or nations such as the Navajo, for example). Knowledge related to the particular community being studied.

Materials: Most important are newspapers, speakers, correspondence with people in the community chosen for study, current "specials" on TV, particularly Public Broadcasting.

Instructional Methods: Research by reading, interviewing, observing. Discussion of issues, problems. Attempts at solving problems by trial and error, thinking through results, referring to authority (experts in the field, not the teacher).

Cognitive Objectives: Reading for information. Categorizing information. Writing reports, letters. Interviewing, questioning. Know the organization of the community studied, understand the need for organization.

Affective Objectives: To feel the difficulties in regulating organized groups. To know that information is needed to solve problems. To understand both sides of an issue—at least to know there are various sides to an issue. To realize the difficulties in controversies in a democracy that has both majority rule and protection of minority rights.

EXCERPTS FROM COVER LETTER

The particular value in that third grade came from solving a very real playground problem. The boys loved to play soccer and constantly got into fights. I refused to be a policeman or jailer and kept repeating that I was a teacher only. The problem was discussed at the "precinct" level over and over again and the decision most often was to try to make one of their own members a policeman or to use punishment. Of course, none of that worked either. There were squabbles over who was at fault and resentments over the punishments. Besides, there were no real enforcers, since I would not do it. Eventually in exasperation several "precincts" asked for a "town meeting." This went along the usual punitive lines, wanting me to do the dirty work. Finally, however, a little girl, not the brightest by any means, said that it would help if the boys learned the rules of the game. I could have kissed her! We had some sixth-grade boys come in and explain the rules and they also volunteered to referee. This solved the basic problem and everything went very well from then on. I think the class learned a lot from discussing the persistent problem and realizing the difference in the pleasure they had after the solution was found.

I think this technique could be used at many levels, using different subjects.

THE UNIT

I. Goals
  A. To develop a knowledge of how communities are organized.
  B. To understand how special interests within a community can lead to conflict.
  C. To find ways of dealing with conflict.
  D. To enable students to evaluate the various ways conflict can be dealt with.
  E. To select and try out what looks like the best way to deal with the conflict.
  F. To evaluate the results and if they are not satisfactory to try another solution, until the best result occurs.
II. Approach: Plan ahead with children on choice of community to be studied.
  A. Plan well ahead for materials. Of course, books and pamphlets from the library, films, and film strips are all to be used, but much more is needed. Here are some suggestions for gathering materials for the various communities that might be studied:
  City: Subscribe to a newspaper from that city. Try to make contact with a school to correspond with children of the same age level. Obtain maps of the city and state.
  Country: Subscribe to a newspaper or magazine from that country, get material from the embassy in Washington. Try to find a speaker from that country. Even if the newspapers are in a language not known in the class, a great deal of information can be gleaned from them.
  Continent: Much the same as for countries, but more is needed. Correspondence with children from each country would be desirable. Find speakers.
  World: Get information from the United Nations. Contact embassies. Find speakers.
  B. When ready to start the unit: Organize the class according to the type of community to be studied depending on grade level, interests, overall curriculum, needs. If the class becomes a city, it can be organized in wards or precincts (or whatever the local organization is); if a continent, organize into countries; if the world, organize into regions. This unit can apply to any grade level or need. Let the children choose as much as possible the group they will work with; alternatively, they can be divided by rows or clusters of desks. Each group should be given the chance to choose the area it wants to represent. The teacher may have to make the final decision.

III. Activities
    A. Newspaper: Information is gleaned from the newspaper by a small group of children chosen either by the teacher or by the class. This group can change daily or weekly as the group wishes. It can be chosen from the class as a whole, or made up of representatives from each precinct or country, or selected on the basis of the special interest of various children. The job would be to cut out or highlight a variety of items and post them on bulletin boards according to their subject and report to the class.
    B. Hold elections for various offices, such a mayor, governor, president, prime minister, UN Secretary General, city council, legislative bodies, Security Council.
    C. Have each group (precinct, country, etc.) make presentations to the legislative body about needs. This can concern needs of the class itself or needs as discovered about the place being studied. Each group would have to do much research and discussion about these needs or problems. If it is a classroom problem that is being worked on, the tendency is to make the teacher the policeman. The teacher, therefore, must make it clear that this is not possible and decline the "honor."
    D. Call in "experts" as needed either for the above needs and problems or for information needed by any of the groups to help them understand better what is being dealt with. These experts could be from outside, but there are experts on some subjects much closer, like children from upper classes, parents, and other professionals in the school.
    E. Keep minutes and notes of all meetings and transactions. Children should summarize things they have learned for future reference in making presentations, etc.
    F. If foreign countries are being studied, then prices in the newspapers should be translated into United States currency and comparisons made about costs.
    G. Read the literature of any countries being studied. A book may be read aloud, but if there are enough books for every child to read a different one, then there should be some kind of discussion so that others know about the variety of literature.
IV. Culmination of the unit.
    A. An evaluation of what has been learned is of utmost importance.
        1. Factual information will be the easiest to come by since the children will have been making notes about what they have learned. Whatever was learned by the various groups will have to be shared in a variety of ways, such as reports to the class, written or illus-

trated reports on bulletin boards, a compilation of those reports to take home, etc.

2. An examination of the problems that were met, solved, and how satisfactory the solution turned out to be is vital. Looking at the problems not solved and trying to find out why is also very important. The teacher will intervene only when it is important to bring out a vital point, usually using a probing question.

3. A final report should be made by the class as a whole about the ways they found effective for solving problems without fighting. They should try to apply these methods to other situations they know of in school, in their neighborhoods, in their community, country, the world.

B. Sharing the above findings with other classes, the school as a whole, with parents, perhaps even with the newspaper, will help enhance the importance of the work the children have done and the importance of their findings. Children can determine how to make their presentations to make them exciting and to get their primary points across. They can use a wide variety of techniques, such as dramatizations, posters, maps, questionnaires, offering to help other classes, etc.

Global Issues: World Hunger

Hunger is doubtless the most widely experienced human consequence of underdevelopment and the inequitable distribution of the world's wealth. As a major symptom of global injustice, it is one of the problems that can be studied in relation to institutional and behavioral change. While famine sometimes becomes so acute that it receives worldwide media attention, peace education has focused more on chronic hunger and malnutrition as the fundamental reality of millions in the developing world. Exploring the causes, location, and current and proposed responses to the problem of world hunger can provide the basis for a more in-depth study of development and the world economy.

The World Food Day Curriculum by the Office on Global Education of the Church World Service—the relief, development, and refugee arm of the National Council of Churches of Christ in the U.S.A.—is a three-unit curriculum for kindergarten through third grade, fourth through seventh grade, and eighth through twelfth grade. Suited to many subjects, it demonstrates how peace education lessons can be used to teach math skills.

Any curriculum on hunger requires that ethical and value issues be raised. Teachers using this curriculum might extend the value dimension and make the connections between hunger and world peace more explicit. (Materials from the American Friends Service Committee would be helpful in this effort.) Included here is the "4–7 Curriculum"; we recommend it for Grades 5 and 6, because it seems too complex for fourth grade and not substantive enough for seventh. It is a complete, self-contained unit ready for classroom implementation.

SELECTION 10
Curriculum Prepared for World Food Day

Entrant: Office on Global Education
Institution: Church World Service, National Council of Churches of Christ in the U.S.A., 2115 N. Charles Street, Baltimore, MD 21218
Grade Level: 4–7
Subject: The curriculum has been used in math, social studies, home economics, and religion classes.
Concepts:
    1. The interdependence of all peoples.
    2. Hunger is primarily an economic and political problem.
    3. Individuals can influence their world.
Topic: World hunger
Materials: A globe; back issues of *National Geographic*, corn flakes; M&M's; photocopies of a world map [map to be copied is included in the curriculum materials]; a flowering plant; gravel.
Instructional Methods: Lecture, discussion, and experiential elements are included in the curriculum.
Cognitive Objectives:
    1. Know the location and extent of the world's hungry.
    2. Understand the meaning of hunger for those who live it.
    3. Begin to grasp the systems that create hunger.
Affective Objectives:
    1. Enhance appreciation for the lives and hard choices of the world's poor.
    2. Encourage belief that students can act as effective agents in the world.
    3. Communicate they are responsible for one another in an interdependent world.

OBJECTIVES

1. To know that food is the most basic human need: Food comes first.
2. To know the meaning of the words "hunger," "malnutrition," and "starvation."
3. To know the number, percentage, and geographical location of the world's hungry.
4. To understand the idea and identity of the first, second, and third worlds.
5. To know that there's enough food for all. People are hungry because they are poor.
6. To understand that students can make a difference, and to know how to help.

TEACHER BACKGROUND

This curriculum provides a one-period introduction to world hunger. In the presentation of the material that follows, students should be encouraged to speculate (brainstorm) possibilities of fact and action. The content of this curriculum intends to encourage action, not guilt. Your role will be critical not only in conveying information, but in supporting and channeling the students' desire to act.

FACTS ON HAND

Hunger of a chronic nature affects 400 to 800 million people around the world. Choosing the most common estimate of 500 million as a point of reference, this means that 1 out of every 8 people in the world suffers from hunger.

Hunger (not getting enough to eat) and malnutrition (not getting the right things to eat) lead to the death of 40,000 children a day (approximately 15 million a year). That's equal to all the children under 15 of California, New York, Illinois, and Texas.

Hunger and malnutrition not only kill, they also maim through brain damage, sterility, and other permanent physical defects. For example, 250,000 people, mostly children, go blind each year due to vitamin deficiency.

Though crop failures, flood, and other natural disasters contribute to hunger, they are not its root cause. There is enough food to eat in the world, but people can't afford to buy it. The root cause of hunger is poverty.

For more information, bibliographies, and curriculum material, write to the National Committee for World Food Day, 1776 F Street N.W., Washington, DC 20437.

LESSON PLAN

Preparation

1. Explain a week before that Food Day is coming. Ask if anyone has heard of it. Inform the students that on October 16 people all over the world will be learning more about food and hunger.

2. Ask students to start collecting pictures and articles on food and hunger in the United States and other countries and to bring those to class October 16.

3. In front of the class take a flowering plant (suggested varieties include Impatiens, Petunias, Hydrangea, Potenella, dwarf Spirea) and repot it in gravel. Inform the students that you're going to water it with a thimble full of water a day and feed it with crushed corn flakes. Ask the students how well they think it will grow and why. Tell them to keep an eye on the plant through the coming week.

On Food Day

1. Explain that today is Food Day. Locate your position on a globe and tell the students that boys and girls all over the globe are also learning about food and hunger today.

2. Ask students how important they think food is, and what other needs they have. Be sure to distinguish needs from wants. Emphasize that of such needs as shelter, clothing, etc., food is the most important. Food comes first.

3. Ask them to decorate a bulletin board with their pictures and clippings supplemented by other pictures you have found from the *National Geographic* illustrating eating and hunger in the United States and around the world.

4. Ask students what it's like to be hungry. How have they felt? Distinguish between not having all you want (a snack) and not getting all you need (hunger/malnutrition). Note the state of the repotted plant. It is suffering from *hunger* (that is, not enough nutrients) and *malnutrition* (the wrong nutrients for health). If this continued, it would die from lack of nutrients — *starvation* — or succumb to a disease. People are the same way.

5. Write 500,000,000 on the board. That's how many hungry people there are in the world. How many is that? Depending on their level of math skills, either have them figure one of the following or tell them for illustration.

a. Estimate the number of M&M's it would take to fill your classroom. There are 27,648 M&M's per cubic foot. (For example, 500 million

M&M's would fill one "typical" 24 $'$ × 41 $'$ × 12 $'$ classroom and one-third of another.)

b. If you started counting to 500 million, counting a number each second (give an example) you would be _____ years old when you were finished (15.85 years plus the student's present age).

c. 500 million inches equals 7,891 miles, approximately equal to the distance between Los Angeles and Darwin, Australia (7,835 miles), New York and Calcutta (7,921 miles), or Denver and Hong Kong (7,465 miles). Be sure to use a globe to illustrate this.

6. Where are the hungry? Explain that most of the hungry in the world live in specific areas. Distribute copies of the world map. Ask students to locate Central America, South America, Africa, the Middle East, and Southeast Asia. Help them with this if necessary. This area comprises the "Third World." Help students identify the Soviet Union and Eastern Europe, known as the "Second World." Locate North America, Western Europe, Australia, and Japan, known as the "First World." It is people in the Third World that comprise the majority of the world's hungry. As the map notes, this division is largely a North/South division.

7. People are hungry mainly because they are poor.[1] That inequity can be illustrated in the following way: The Third World, which has 74% of the people in the world, has only 26% of the world's wealth. The Second World, with 9% of the world's population, has 18% of the world's wealth; and the First World, with 17% of the world's population, has 56% of the world's wealth.[2] The majority of those living in the Third World live very poorly. To illustrate what that's like, read *Living on $200 a Year* (depending on the class, this may require some paraphrasing). Then ask your students to draw a picture of such a life with their own family in it. It may be helpful to make this inequity more vivid by dividing your class into appropriate proportions and distributing M&M's according to the equivalent wealth percentages.

8. Emphasize that people all over the world are trying to work to make their lives better and to help those who are poor to improve their situation. There are ways in which they can help:

a. Contact your local United Nations Association, UNICEF, or a private voluntary agency (CARE, Church World Service, etc.) for suggestions on how to raise funds for their efforts to feed the hungry.

b. Start a garden. Ask your students to plant a garden, care for it, and then either eat the food, give the food away, or sell the food and take the money earned and give it to an organization helping to feed the hungry.

---

[1]This is the case for the hungry in the First World as well as the Third World. Students should not be left with the impression that hunger does not exist in the First World — Ed.

[2]It might also be observed that this wealth is produced in some significant part on the basis of "raw materials" or resources from the Third World — Ed.

c. Encourage the students to become recyclers. Perhaps organize a recycling drive.
d. Have the students organize a poster contest for the school on world hunger and place the posters around the school on parents' night.
e. The students may wish to organize a Thanksgiving food drive.
f. Organize an educational program on hunger with students giving talks, skits, and presentations and present this to other classes or perhaps to some parents on parents' night.
g. Encourage the students to talk with their families about what they've learned.
h. Encourage the students to write to their local congressional representative and senator and the president about what they've learned. The appropriate addresses are:
Congressperson _____, U.S. House of Representatives, Washington, DC 20515
Senator _____, U.S. Senate Office Building, Washington, DC 20510.
President _____, The White House, Washington, DC 20500.

Learning to Know and Love the Planet:
Environmental Studies as a Basis for Peace Education

If a commitment to life is to be a fundamental value and affective learning objective upon which we base peace education, then knowledge of the planet that sustains life has to be a primary cognitive objective. From the very beginnings of formal education children need to learn about the Earth and the various life forms it has produced. Such objectives should be central to science education, and science curricula based on such objectives are most certainly suitable for peace education.

A commitment to life is the basic value objective of an elementary science program being developed by the Educational Program of Shelburne Farms. Its purposes are environmental and ecological education, an integral component of education for positive peace. The central norm of the value system the program espouses is stewardship, one of the three primary concepts of the recommended comprehensive program for peace education. Conservation of natural resources is the "behavioral objective" based on that norm. The assumptions which underlie the objective explicate the philosophy of the Shelburne Farms program. A number of them coincide with the assumptions with which we began the curriculum survey and developed the concepts and guidelines for the comprehensive program. We have excerpted the assumptions, the concepts, and the topics to serve as guidelines for science teachers who also seek to teach the concept of stewardship and an understanding of the ecological imperatives of Planet Earth.

SELECTION 11
K–6 Science Topics

Contact person: Dr. David Barash, Director of Education, Shelburne Farms, Shelburne, VT 05482

ASSUMPTIONS

In order to most effectively reach the stated goal of conservation of natural resources, Shelburne Farms is working with these base assumptions:

1. Education is a pro-active, long-term change agent and, hence, is an appropriate vehicle to encourage the building of a conservation ethic.

2. The most efficient way for Shelburne Farms to reach its goal is to identify and take advantage of the main points of highest "learning leverage." In the case of students, the teacher is in this role.

3. The most effective way to achieve a positive educational effect is to work, for the most part, through pre-existing educational structures.

4. Children learn best through tactile experiences (à la John Dewey) and education that uses this type of learning is inherently a motivating vehicle to achieve the learning objectives set forth by the educational system at large (i.e., schools, etc.).

5. Teachers are likely to use educational techniques that achieve the learning objectives for their students if those teachers find the techniques simple to use, motivating for the students, and pedagologically correct.

6. Each season offers an abundance of learning opportunities and those learning opportunities can be developed in such a way that they teach not only the learning objectives, but in addition encourage an awareness of the natural systems that are manifested in the seasons.

7. Over the long term, awareness on the part of the child learner leads to understanding, which in turn leads to affinity, all of which build an ethic of stewardship toward natural resources by the time the child has become an adult.

8. We live in a world whose resources are humanly managed, and the production of food and fiber perfectly exemplifies the intersection of people and the use of natural resources for basic needs.

9. Resource use is, for the most part, different seasonally, and in each region of the country and the world there exists a different set of cultural interactions, as dictated by the seasons and the respective dominant natural resources (i.e., sugaring time in New England, cotton harvest in the South, etc.).

10. If assumptions 1–9 are taken to be correct, there is a niche within the current educational system that is based on those assumptions. Furthermore, that this niche is currently strong is due to recent trends in education pertaining to the identification of science and math as needing to be strengthened.

11. This niche does exist, and it is unfilled — though how big a niche is undetermined.

12. The education program developed at Shelburne Farms is of high quality, successful, and transferable, and can successfully fill that niche.

SUGGESTED SCOPE AND SEQUENCE OF TOPICS

Life Science	*Earth Science*	*Physical Science*
K–1	*K–1*	*K–1*
Growing seeds	Season awareness	Matter changes
Grouping animals	Weather	Magnets
Using Senses	Light and shadow	
Introduction to the life cycle of plants and animals	Weather and seasonal changes	
	Our sun and our moon	
2–3	*2–3*	*2–3*
Characteristics of living and non-living things	Rocks	Basic properties of air
Changes in the life cycles of animals	Things in the sky	Some sources of light
Communities of living things	Solar system	Sound
	Changes in the earth's surface	Doing work
4–5	*4–5*	*4–5*
Pollution and conservation	Minerals, rocks, and fossils	Light and optics
Life in the sea	Exploring the universe	Matter all around
Green plant systems	Environmental aspects of earth science	Electricity and magnets
Food/energy		

Life Science	*Earth Science*	*Physical Science*
6	*6*	*6*
Bacteria and molds	Earth history	Solar energy
	Solid earth (geology)	Introduction to simple machines
	Dynamic earth (energy in core)	
	Atmosphere and weather	
	Oceanography	

SECTION III
Junior High School Grades (7–9)

Critical Capacities: Training Skills for Making Judgments and Taking Stands

As young peacemakers grow from childhood toward adolescence and more formal citizenship education, their knowledge of and attitudes toward the world should develop in complexity and breadth. They need to become fully aware of the broad range of human differences, ideological as well as cultural. The concepts of interdependence and multiculturalism can be applied as a framework for their growing knowledge of conflicts and problems. Their views of social responsibility should come to include a global perspective and a sense of interdependence with the planet and all of its peoples. They should begin to exercise their critical, reflective capacities to analyze problems and propose solutions. Indeed, through approaching problems in a rational fashion youngsters of this age can confront their fears.

Critical and analytic thinking are skills that most secondary peace educators seek to develop. As indicated in the previous section, we believe the process should begin even earlier. The ability to think rationally about issues of war and injustice is especially essential to a field in which the central questions are so obscured by misinformation and controversy and so clouded with fear and other strong emotional responses. Developing the capacity to formulate personal opinions and make independent decisions requires well-developed thinking skills. The specific thinking skills required are featured by the Peace Links Curriculum (see Selection 13).

Global citizenship education at the stage of pre-adolescence, ages 12–14, should offer students opportunities to reflect upon individual and collective social responsibility, pro-active stewardship, and ethical decision making. Within this context of education for participation in the democratic process, introducing questions related to nuclear weapons and war would now be appropriate. Information about specific issues such as those related to understanding the Soviet Union (Selection 14) and the problems of military expenditures (Selection 15) can be introduced at this level. As students come to understand the true nature of global problems and become aware of

51

possibilities for constructive action, they will be more likely to feel empowered to confront the nuclear challenge.

Planetary Stewardship: Affirming Life

The concept of the planet as a living organism, a set of interdependent, natural systems interacting with human systems, can be introduced at this stage as the basis for a more mature and active notion of Earth stewardship. Respect for the living Earth and responsibility for the health of the planet are the main values deriving from this concept, which, as exemplified by Rainbow Sign Curriculum (Selection 12), rest upon the primary fundamental value of life. Therefore, as its primary fundamental affective learning objectives at this stage, peace education seeks to cultivate a commitment to life, its preservation, the improvement of its quality, and the opening of its opportunities to all the human family.

The following excerpts were selected as materials that stress stewardship, global responsibility, cross-cultural understanding, and problem solving.

Stewardship: Caring for the Earth

Love of the Earth as giver of life is deeply rooted in many human cultures. In our society, however, the roots have been paved over by layers of asphalt and concrete—products of a techno-industrial culture that has denied the breathing, living character of the planet. The value of stewardship flowers mainly in "traditional" societies and in those instances when we uncover some of our own deep cultural roots, as is the case with "The Rainbow Curriculum."

This curriculum was written for use in Jewish religious education by Judith Axler and David Harbater. We see it as having applicability as well to religious education in other denominations, to environmental education, and/or to the study of Western culture. Whether viewed as ancient history, revelation, or as a myth to provide meaning to our culture, the story of the Flood has much to teach contemporary generations of all faiths. Through this story lessons can be fashioned about the living Earth, human relationship to and responsibility for it, and the problems posed by ecological destruction and the threat of nuclear holocaust.

This curriculum could also be used to initiate discussion of the traditions and myths of other cultures regarding humanity's relationship to the Earth. It has potential for cross-cultural as well as comparative-religions approaches to environment and peace issues and questions of ecological responsibility. The issues it raises in terms of "the covenant" are essentially ethical issues for all human societies in the techno-industrial nuclear age and can be used to initiate some essential inquiry into the moral choicemaking that will determine the future of the Earth.

This unit has been chosen to open the section on junior high school curricula because it is an appropriate introduction to the issue of nuclear weapons. While teachers should be prepared to deal with children's concerns with and interest in possibilities for nuclear war from the earliest levels of schooling, the school should refrain from initiating study of these problems until the "pre-adolescent" stage of preparing for adult responsibilities. "The Fate of the Earth" as the overarching issue of the end of the twentieth century is the most appropriate one with which to begin specific study for global citizenship, the major contemporary social responsibility.

SELECTION 12
The Rainbow Sign: A Jewish Curriculum for the Nuclear Age

Entrant: David Harbater (co-author: Judith Axler)*
School: University of Pennsylvania, Department of Mathematics, Philadelphia, PA 19104-3859
   This curriculum has been used in private, Jewish schools in the Philadelphia area.
Grade Level: 3–8
Subject: Jewish Religious Studies Concepts: The Biblical Flood of Noah, and the Rainbow Covenant that followed, in which God and humanity each took on responsibilities toward preserving the Earth and the survival of the species. These are viewed as a focus regarding our responsibilities toward preventing war (especially nuclear) and preserving the environment.
Topics: The Flood and Rainbow Covenant; the extent to which we have lived up to the covenant; the Earth as ark; Nuclear War as the Flood; historical lessons; what we can do.
Materials: The curriculum consists of 11 pages, including a bibliography of suggested resources.
Instructional Methods: Presentation of material; questions asked of students; directed class discussion.
Cognitive Objectives: Knowledge of the Flood story from the perspective of the Rainbow Covenant; skills of seeing connections between familiar

---

*The authors wish to acknowledge their debt to Arthur Waskow of the Shalom Center, who developed many of the ideas expressed in this curriculum.

stories and the outside world; understanding that the world can be and has been changed (for better and for worse) by the actions of human beings.

Affective Objectives: Desire to act so as to make the world a better place (more peaceful, better environmentally, etc.), and belief in the possibility that such action is possible. A "one-world" perspective, as opposed to an "us vs. them" perspective. A perspective in which the religious ideals of peace and preservation of the Earth are valued as important in everyday life.

INTRODUCTION

This curriculum is an attempt to provide a Jewish approach to what has been called "Nuclear Age Education." It draws on the notion of Rainbow Sign: Noah's Flood and the covenant that followed. By this approach, it seeks to draw upon Jewish traditions and values, and to balance the message of warning with one of hope. In emphasizing the need for us to uphold our part of the covenant—for us to act in ways that preserve the Earth—we point out the possibility, and the necessity, that we "choose life."

Overview of this curriculum.   For the world today, faced by a nuclear peril, the story of the Flood takes on new significance. The Flood story is not just one of destruction, though, but also one of hope, because of the Rainbow Covenant. We should remind ourselves of the covenant, and of humanity's responsibility to uphold our part. We have not always done so. But we can do better. And what we choose to do can make a difference—as our tradition and history teach us. In addition, the Flood story has other concepts to offer: the image of nuclear holocaust as "Flood," rather than as "war"; the image of our planet today as like the ark, alone and adrift, surrounded by emptiness, and inhabited by a diverse population forced to live together; the image of Noah building the ark out in the open, in an attempt to warn others of an impending peril that could still be averted. This curriculum seeks to focus students' attention on these ideas, through class discussion and (for younger students) an art project.

How to use this curriculum.   This curriculum contains a version of the presentations and discussion that first took place in about ten classrooms in the spring of 1984. The students varied in age from 8 to 15, and the presentations varied accordingly.

THE FLOOD STORY

In telling the story, break up the narrative now and then by asking leading questions of the students. (For example: How does the ark symbolize the importance of species preservation? What day did the Rainbow appear? What is a "covenant"? Who were the parties to this covenant? What did God agree to do? What is our obligation? When we see a rainbow, what should we remember?) Here is a sample narrative:

We read in Genesis that there was violence and corruption in the world, and God was sorry that he had ever created the world. So he decided to destroy it by a Flood, and to start over. He told Noah to build an ark for himself and his family and for two of each species of life, so that after the Flood there would be survivors to start the world over.

One day in the spring, on the seventeenth day of the Hebrew month of Iyar, the Flood started. It rained for forty days and forty nights, and everything was wiped out — except for Noah and his family, and the animals he brought on the ark. Even after the rain stopped, the Earth was still covered with water.

But finally, a year and ten days after the Flood began (Which day? the 27th of Iyar), the Earth was dry, and Noah and his family and all the animals left the ark. God put a rainbow in the sky, to signify his covenant with Noah (What's a "covenant"?), promising never again to destroy all life on Earth. And he said that from then on, he'd put a rainbow in the sky after it rained, to remind himself and us of the covenant. (Any time *we* see a rainbow, we're reminded that *this* rain is a good rain — a rain of life, for us, for the crops, for the animals — not a rain of destruction, which God has promised never again to send.) But if a covenant is a bargain, a contract, then who is it between? (God and Noah, with Noah representing all of us.) Just as God promised not to destroy the Earth, what is *our* part of the bargain? (We're to act as caretakers of life on Earth. Human beings have a special role to play on Earth, but at the same time there are limits to what we're allowed to do. By violating these limits, the people of Noah's time had brought the Flood on themselves.)

DISCUSSION

Have we lived up to our part of the covenant?   Ask the students: Have we helped to preserve the Earth and life on Earth? Have we acted as caretakers, recognizing limits on our actions? In what ways have we? In what ways haven't we?

An Outline for the Discussion

1. We've acted in ways that have destroyed many forms of life. Even after surviving the Flood, these species have become extinct in recent times. One example is the dodo bird, and now we have the expression that something is "as dead as a dodo." Other species are now close to becoming extinct. But at least we're now doing what we can to save them, before it's too late. One example is the whooping crane. Another is the bald eagle, our national bird. There used to be lots of bald eagles, but now there are only a few. As long as some are left, it's still possible to save them—but once they're all gone, it's too late. So it's important to act now. After all, each time we make a species extinct, we violate the covenant, and we destroy a little bit of the world.

2. We've wasted many of our natural resources, acting as though there would always be more of everything. And we've polluted the environment, poisoning some water supplies, making the air unhealthful to breath, and sometimes even poisoning a whole town, so that it's dangerous for anyone to stay (like Times Beach, MO, contaminated by dioxin). But in recent years, people have been more aware of this, and have been trying to protect the environment.

3. We've again filled the world with violence—in people's daily lives, on the streets of our cities, and on battlefields around the world. Too often we're quick to pick a fight instead of working together to understand each other's point of view. And countries do the same thing. There are now wars going on in many parts of the world—in Latin America, in Africa, in Asia. Meanwhile, the most powerful countries in the world are building more and more nuclear weapons. And if *they are* ever used, then the whole world could be destroyed. Until recently, we could only violate the covenant a little bit at a time; but with nuclear weapons, we have the ability to violate it completely. It's a tragedy whenever any *one* species becomes extinct; how much more so, if *all* the species were to become extinct, at once.

LESSONS FROM THE FLOOD STORY

The Earth as ark.   The Earth today is in some ways like Noah's ark. The ark was a big place—it had to be, to hold all those animals. But is was also a small place—a single boat, out at sea, surrounded by nothing but water. Those on board had to make do with what they had, because there was nothing outside. Imagine if they tossed their garbage around the ark or threw away things after using them just once. Soon they wouldn't have the things they needed, and the ark wouldn't be a livable place. It's the same with us. If we pollute and use up our resources, we're also in trouble. Our planet is like an ark, and outside it is the emptiness of space. We'd better make sure the earth is a livable place, because we have no other place to go.

The Earth is also like the ark in another way.   Imagine if some of the animals on the ark didn't get along with some of the other animals. Maybe the elephants and the giraffes argued and blamed each other for everything that went wrong on the ark. What if they began fighting with each other? How would it soon be for all the others on board? Imagine if the elephants thought to themselves, "We'll fix those giraffes. When they're not looking, we'll take our drill, and bore a hole in the bottom of *their* side of the ark." What then? (The entire ark would sink, of course.) And what if both the elephants *and* the giraffes had drills? Would the elephants become safer if they got more and bigger drills? Or if instead they began to communicate with the giraffes, and tried to understand each other's point of view? Maybe they'd never be best of friends, but at least if they understood each other they'd be better able to live together, rather than destroying the whole ark.

We're in much the same situation today. The United States and the Soviet Union are rivals and perhaps will never see eye to eye. Both have thousands of nuclear weapons. Meanwhile, scientists tell us that if even a small fraction of these weapons are used — say half the weapons on one side and none of those on the other — then all life on earth could be destroyed. After all the explosions, and the firestorms, and the radiation, and the destruction of the cities and hospitals — after all that, there could be a nuclear winter: The sky would become dark, the rivers would freeze, the crops would die, and the world would no longer be a place to support life. Let's ask ourselves: Are we safer if both sides build more weapons? Or if both sides make an effort to understand each other better, and to live together despite disagreements?

Nuclear war as Flood (for older students).   The image the Torah presents us with of worldwide destruction is not that of a war, but of a Flood. This gives us a new way to think about the nuclear peril — that the danger is of a nuclear "flood of fire" rather than of a "war" in the usual sense. After all, a war is something fought between two sides to achieve certain goals, and one side agrees to stop fighting after deciding that the costs of continuing to fight are greater than the costs of giving in. But a "nuclear war" is different. Afterwards, there are no winners. And, if we are all destroyed, there are no losers either. This is not a "war." It is more like the Flood, an event which was brought on by the actions of those people who lived in Noah's time, and which destroyed those people.

As long as we continue to think about nuclear holocaust as a "war," we remain trapped in an endless arms race, in a desperate attempt to find "security." But if we — and people in other nations — can change this perspective, there may be another way. As Einstein said, in the Nuclear Age, "we shall require a substantially new manner of thinking if mankind is to survive."

The ark as warning (for older students).   Noah was told to build his ark in the open. Why? To serve as a warning to others. Had they listened, and changed, then the Flood would have been averted. Instead, people ridiculed Noah, the Flood came, and they perished. Today, those who are concerned about dangers to the Earth have a responsibility to warn others. There is the possibility that those doing so will be ridiculed. But it is important to bring the situation to the attention of others, so that there can be a change before it is too late.

DISCUSSION

What can we do to uphold the covenant?   Ask for suggestions from the class. Here are some possible responses:

1. The first step in fulfilling the covenant is for us to ask ourselves, *Are we fulfilling the covenant?* Are we doing what we can in our everyday lives? How do we react to disagreements with our friends and neighbors: by turning to violence, or by working to resolve things peacefully? Are we wasteful and are we litterbugs, or do we care about our environment? Do we act ethically, or in a corrupt manner? By being aware of this question, we can begin to live more peaceful lives in which we cherish the Earth and life on Earth. Imagine how different the world would be if all people, Jews and non-Jews, kept the Rainbow Covenant in mind and did their best to observe it.

2. In working to observe the covenant, we can act not only as individuals but also as members of society. In our democratic society, we all have a role to play, and we have a responsibility to take part. For example, we can write letters to the editor of our newspaper, and letters to our elected officials, describing our concerns about the environment, about species extinction, and about the nuclear threat. And after turning eighteen, we all have a right and a duty to vote. But when voting or writing letters, we should be expressing informed opinions. So it's important for us to study and learn more about these issues. (And after all, Judaism values learning as one of the highest pursuits.) We can do this by reading, and by discussion with parents, teachers, friends, and others in our communities. In these discussions we can also help others to learn more and to think about these problems. (Remember Noah building the ark out in the open in his community.)

3. We can also help to keep the Rainbow Covenant in mind by observing its anniversary each year during the Rainbow Sign period, from the 17th to the 27th of Iyar. During that period we should recall the covenant, and should rededicate ourselves to it — through discussions, song, prayer, study, and activities. And we can remember the covenant by saying the traditional blessing when we see a rainbow:

> Blessed art thou, Lord our God, King of the universe, who remembers the covenant, and keeps your promise faithfully.

RESOURCES

Preventing the Nuclear Holocaust: A Jewish Response, edited by Rabbi David Saperstein. Available for $5.95 from the UAHC Religious Action Center, 2027 Massachusetts Ave. NW, Washington, DC 20036.

Keeping Posted, 28(1), October 1982. "Choose Life." Contact UAHC, 838 Fifth Avenue, New York, NY 10021. (212) 249-0100.

Menorah: Sparks of Jewish Renewal, published monthly. Subscriptions: $24/year, from P.O. Box 1308V, Ft. Lee, NJ 07024. There are back issues about Rainbow Sign.

Sukkot Shalom, peace curricula drawing on themes of Sukkot. Contact the Shalom Center, Church Rd. & Greenwood Ave., Wyncote, PA 19095. (212) 576-0800.

Introductory Guide: Jewish Nuclear Education. Available in draft form from JESR, 50 Verndale St., Brookline, MA 02146. (617) 735-0734.

Rainbow Covenant Workbook. Contact UAHC Northeast Council, 1330 Beacon St., Suite 355, Brookline, MA 02146. (617) 277-1655.

NFTY Against the Arms Race, by Rabbi Ramie Adrian with Adam Lipton. NFTY Resources, Glen Way, Syosset, NY 11701, order #S31. $3.

Jewish Roots of Non-violence. Available from Jewish Peace Fellowship, Box 271, Nyack, NY 10960. (914) 358-4601.

Dialogue: A Teaching Guide to Nuclear Issues. Educators for Social Responsibility, 23 Garden St., Cambridge, MA 02138. (617) 492-1764. $12.95.

The Nuclear Winter, an illustrated pamphlet by scientist Carl Sagan. Available free from Council for a Liveable World Education Fund, 11 Beacon St., Boston, MA 02108.

[Editor's Note: Another set of resources for teachers using this curriculum in religious education are the many Christian denominational statements on nuclear weapons and the arms race. A list of such statements is available from United Ministries in Education and from COPRED (see Resource Organizations). An additional source on the Jewish perspectives is

Bradley Artson, *A Jewish Consideration of War and Nuclear Conflict* (New York: United Synagogues of America, 1986)].

Critical and Creative Thinking:
Dealing with Fears, Controversy, and the Future

Peace Links, an organization founded by Betty Bumpers, is headquartered in Little Rock, Arkansas, the state represented in the United States Senate by her husband, Dale Bumpers. The following curriculum has been taken into local schools by some members of Peace Links who are experienced educators. Peace Links has prepared a variety of materials dealing with various dimensions of peace education, such as lessons on holidays or heroes.

Their material on "Thinking Skills" is available in two versions, one for middle schools and one for secondary schools. The middle school unit appears in this section as an example of how to start the critical thinking process in the junior high school grades. Both versions are directed toward the development of the same skills, rational thinking, analyzing complex issues, understanding negotiations, and creative thinking. The last exercise is essentially a brainstorming technique within the parameters of an inquiry marked out by a particular set of questions. The questions are well formulated to help students develop the essential peacemaking skill of thinking in terms of alternatives. It brings an important cognitive dimension to the capacity for creative imagination awakened by the simpler forms of imaging recommended for the elementary grades (see Selections 5 and 6).

The first three skills contribute to the development of problem-solving capacities in the human experience. The fourth is based upon the assumption that the unprecedented nature of global problems of nuclear war demands creative, new ways of thinking, an assumption expressed in the four significant quotations appearing on the cover page of the unit.

SELECTION 13
Thinking Skills for the Nuclear Age

Entrant: Barbara Stanford
Institution: Peace Links, 12406 Colleen Drive, Little Rock, AR 72212 (home address of the author)
Grade Level: 6–8
Department or Subject Area: Social Studies or English
Concepts: The nuclear age requires new thinking skills.

Topics:
   Dealing with emotions
   Point of view
   Negotiation
   Imagining a world without war
Instructional Methods:
   Discussion
   Role play
Cognitive Objectives:
   1. Seeing alternative points of view
   2. Creating a new vision
   3. Generating alternative resolutions to a conflict.
Affective Objectives: Using emotions healthfully.

MIDDLE SCHOOL VERSION

The unleashed power of the atom has changed everything except our ways
of thinking.
                                                        Albert Einstein

The central problem of our time — as I view it — is how to employ human
intelligence for the salvation of mankind. Have we already gone too far in
this search for peace through the accumulation of peril? Is there anyway to
halt this trend . . . ? I believe there is a way out. And I believe it because I
have acquired in my lifetime a decent respect for human intelligence.
                                                  General Omar Bradley

Our future on this planet, exposed as it is to nuclear annihilation, depends
upon one single factor: humanity must make a moral about-face. At the
present moment of history, there must be a general mobilization of all men
and women of goodwill. Humanity is called upon to take a major step
forward, a step forward in civilization and wisdom.
                                                     Pope John Paul II

The world has become a more crowded, more interconnected, more volatile
and unstable place. If education cannot help students see beyond themselves and better understand the interdependent nature of our world, each
new generation will remain ignorant and its capacity to live confidently and
responsibly will be dangerously diminished.
                 Carnegie Report on Secondary Education in America

   Peace Links has prepared the following resources and activities to help
teachers prepare their students to think critically and creatively about the

major issues of the nuclear age. These activities are designed not to encourage students to accept any particular point of view or position on nuclear issues, but rather to educate them to analyze and evaluate issues on their own. Specific proposals and political positions will probably change considerably by the time today's students begin to vote, but the problems of controlling nuclear weapons on a small, interdependent planet will still be major concerns.

The problems of the nuclear age require certain kinds of thinking skills which have not been emphasized in the past. The first problem most people meet in dealing with the nuclear issue is that fears of nuclear war are so deeply rooted that many people are unable or unwilling to think about the issue at all. Those who do begin to think about it discover that the issue is so complex that their old methods of analyzing an issue do not seem to work. Not only are the facts about weapons systems overwhelming, but the concepts and techniques and even vocabulary of negotiation are unfamiliar. As a result, little creative thinking is done about the issue.

OBJECTIVES

Four major mental skills are needed to think effectively about the problems of the nuclear age. This unit contains activities to help students reach the following four objectives:

1. Students will learn to recognize when fears are influencing their thinking and will learn ways of handling their fears so that they can think rationally about the issue.
2. Students will learn techniques of analysis that are helpful in studying an issue as complex as nuclear war.
3. Students will learn basic concepts and techniques of negotiation.
4. Students will learn creative thinking techniques that are useful for thinking of new solutions to complex problems.

SKILL ONE: THINKING WITH OUR MINDS INSTEAD OF OUR FEARS

If your students want to talk a lot about nuclear war or do not want to talk about it at all, they are probably reacting to the topic with their fears and emotions rather than with their minds. If they become overemotional in discussions and make exaggerated statements such as "Just one nuclear bomb would destroy the whole world," or "We're all going to die from nuclear war so there's no need to think about it," they need to cope with their feelings before they can think rationally.

The following materials available from Peace Links may be useful:

Bombs Will Make the Rainbow Break. Zahum-Hurwitz production. A 30-minute film about children 10 to 14 years old. Through their artwork and words it tries to communicate what it is like growing up in a world threatened by nuclear war.

In the Nuclear Shadow. This film has a positive message. The counterpart to fear is action. The children in this film are of various races and backgrounds. They emphasize that the way to overcome, or at least lessen, the feelings of despair and defenselessness, is through personal involvement.

Peace Panels. Panels of four speakers from various segments of the community who tell their personal experience of becoming aware of the threat of nuclear war and overcoming their fears to the point that they could think rationally about them.

What to Tell the Children. A packet of readings on children and the nuclear threat.

SKILL TWO: THINKING CRITICALLY ABOUT COMPLEX ISSUES

If your students are confused by widely conflicting reports on the effects of nuclear war, or if they tend to suggest simplistic solutions, the following materials and activities may be useful. These activities can be adapted to a study of any complex, controversial issue and may be helpful to students who refuse to listen to anyone who disagrees with them on any topic.

Activity: Seeing from Different Points of View

Collect and display cartoons of people arguing. Ask students to explain what the people in the cartoons saw different in the situations. Why did they see things differently?

Activity: Seeing from Another Country's Point of View

Ask students to choose an article in the newspaper about a country that is arguing or fighting with the United States. Draw a cartoon showing how Americans see the problem and then draw how the people of the other country probably see the problem.

Activity: Summarizing an Argument You Disagree With

Ask students to number their papers from 1 to 5 and for each statement you read, to write either A for agree, D for disagree, or N for no opinion.

1. The best way of preventing nuclear war is to have a stronger military force than the Soviet Union.
2. Religion really provides the only answer to the nuclear dilemma.
3. Arms control agreements are not worth much because the Russians will violate them.
4. I don't think anybody will survive an all-out nuclear war.
5. If we are going to survive in the nuclear age we have to learn to understand and cooperate with the Russians.

After everyone has finished, assign students to a partner who disagreed with them on at least one of the statements. Assign each person to ask the partner to explain his or her beliefs and the reasons for them. Tell them to keep asking questions until they really understand why their partners believe as they do. Then tell them to write a paper explaining the other person's point of view. You may need to remind students that they are not to argue or try to convince the other person, but simply to take turns communicating their point of view and trying to understand the other point of view.

Activity: Seeing Alternatives

1. Select and distribute a newspaper account of a problem or issue. Have students either individually, in groups, or as a whole class brainstorm alternative approaches to it. The rules of brainstorming are:
   a. Every idea should be listed no matter how bad or silly. The goal is simply to get as many ideas as possible.
   b. No reactions or comments should be made about ideas until the brainstorming process is over.
2. After you have all of the ideas listed, go back over the list and try to figure out what the consequences of each alternative might be. After you have looked at all of the possible consequences, decide which alternative is best.

SKILL THREE: UNDERSTANDING THE PROCESS OF NEGOTIATION

Negotiations, treaties, and talks are widely suggested as ways of ending or controlling the arms race. Yet few citizens have very extensive understandings of the process of negotiations, how it works or what strategies are likely to be successful. As a result, citizens often have unrealistic expectations about negotiation, expecting quick, easy agreements in a process that often takes years.

For young people, the easiest way to learn the basic concepts of negotiation is to begin by studying interpersonal conflict resolution. A student manual for learning conflict resolution skills and concepts is available from Peace Links.

There are some major differences between interpersonal negotiation and international negotiation. If you use the conflict resolution booklets, you may need to point out some of the following major differences. In international negotiations, since trust is usually low, both sides usually try to hide their weaknesses and to start by making high demands. In international negotiations, the negotiators also rarely have full power to make decisions. Their decisions must be ratified by people back home, and often there are several factions who must be satisfied.

The following materials are useful for teaching about negotiation (consult Educators for Social Responsibility for purchase information).

> *Perspectives: A Teaching Guide to Concepts of Peace.* A 400-page teacher's guide with detailed lessons for Grades K–12 on concepts of peace, obstacles to peace, conflict resolution, peacemakers, and imagining the future. Copies may be borrowed from the Peace Links office or ordered for $12.95 from Educators for Social Responsibility (see Resource Organizations).
>
> *Firebreaks.* A fairly complex simulation of negotiations between the United States and the Soviet Union during a nuclear crisis. It teaches concepts of negotiation as well as giving participants a chance to play the roles. It would take 3–5 days of class time.
>
> *Peacemaking 1814.* A computer simulation teaching skills of negotiation using the negotiations to end the War of 1812. Can be used by a whole class for a two-day lesson or played by individuals. Programmed for Apple IIe. Available from the Peace Links.

SKILL FOUR: CREATIVE THINKING

Because nuclear war is a relatively new situation, the solutions to nuclear war are likely to be different from our previous experiences. Creative thinking skills are therefore useful. The following films available from Peace Links may be useful, as well as the two attached activities.

> *No Frames, No Boundaries.* A 21-minute film available from the Peace Links office. It was made by Creative Initiatives and takes its theme from the perspective of astronaut Russel Schweickart as he stepped into space during the Apollo 9 flight. It shows the evolution of the limitations of boundaries and the dangers that they

create today. Designed to encourage creative approaches to the
problem rather than to suggest solutions.

Beyond War. A 20-minute videotape available from the Peace Links
office in which Americans from a wide range of backgrounds
discuss the idea that we must move beyond war as a means of
coping with conflicts.

Creative Thinking Activity

Hand out or read aloud the unfinished story, "A Voyage to Arret."
Have each student complete the story as they wish with writing, drawings or
dramatizations.

A Voyage to Arret

We didn't think we were going to a new planet when our class was
selected by NASA to be the first students to go into space. We were
just supposed to orbit Earth a few times doing science experiments and
then return home.

But as we were taking off, something happened. Somehow, all of
the rockets fired at the same time in the wrong direction and before we
knew what had happened, we found ourselves, not orbiting Earth, but
orbiting the sun, heading in the opposite direction from Earth!

We figured that if we kept going, we would eventually meet Earth
on the other side of the sun, but in about half of the time it should
have taken us, we suddenly saw a planet up ahead of us. It looked a lot
like Earth, but it was on the opposite side of the sun, so we called it
Arret, which is Terra, another name for Earth, spelled backwards.

We were surprised and relieved to find that Arret was a lot like
Earth. The people looked a lot like us and some of them even spoke a
language that was almost like English. They had pizza and video-
games.

But some things were a little different. There were two superpowers on Arret, the A.S.U. and the R.S.S.U. The A.S.U. had a government similar to our Democracy and the R.S.S.U. had a system similar
to Communism. But one thing was really different. They didn't have
any nuclear weapons. In fact, they didn't have any war weapons at all.
They didn't even have a word for war in any of their languages. War
had never been invented in Arret!

While the scientists at ASAN were fixing up our spaceship so we
could go home, we decided to explore Arret to see what a planet
without any armies or weapons was like. We wondered how they
protected themselves? What do young people do instead of joining the
army? Without any war, what kind of TV shows do they have? If there

have never been any wars, what did they study in history? How do they keep the communists from taking over the free countries?

We decided to split up to see what a world was like without any war. Some of us went to other countries and some of us just wandered into different places — schools, churches, shopping centers, homes — and talked to people. Some of us even went to visit the President. These are our reports on what a world without war is like. . . .

Now, choose the place you would visit on Arret and finish the story with your own version of what a world without war is like.

Sharing Images of a Warless World

Have students compare their stories. On the board draw up a list of characteristics that a world without war seems to have. Discuss whether or not students think such a world would be possible. Then discuss whether such a world could be created on Earth with our present history. If so, how?

Soviet Studies: Attitudes and Information

While the American public and American foreign policy are excessively preoccupied with the Soviet Union, these preoccupations have not produced much knowledge of its government, its peoples, cultures, history, or any of the factors that determine the Soviet world view and position in world politics. No other single factor has a more profound influence on world peace than the relations between the two "superpowers." It is essential that they know as much as possible about each other. Peace education in the United States should include a serious and thorough study of the Soviet Union. Peace educators should take every opportunity to learn in depth what must be communicated to students. Many are doing so; some even visit the USSR under the sponsorship of peace groups, religious associations or professional organizations such as Educators for Social Responsibility (ESR). One leader of such an ESR visit submitted two complete curricula for teaching about the Soviet Union. Claudia Zaslavsky prepared "Learning About the Soviet Union" for both the middle grades and the secondary grades.

The following excerpts comprise the activities designated for the middle grades. During these years when children begin to reflect on world events and to formulate political and economic attitudes toward other systems, it is important that they have an opportunity to study Soviet society. It is equally important that critical and analytic skills be applied in such study. The Zaslavsky unit does so as it emphasizes social responsibility and active participation in the democratic process. Peace educators seeking to develop their own units on the Soviet Union will find Zaslavsky's resource list is very useful.

SELECTION 14
Learning About the Soviet Union

Entrant: Claudia Zaslavsky

Institution: Educators for Social Responsibility/Metro, 490 Riverside Drive, New York, NY 10027

Grade Level: 6–9

Subject: Social studies; can also involve language arts.

Concepts: Critical thinking to make decisions about Soviet–U.S. relations, to overcome attitudes toward and images of the Soviet Union based on stereotypes and insufficient information; acquisition of information on which judgments can be based; investigation of the "other side," Soviet views on arms control and relations with the United States.

Topics: Geographical and historical information about the Soviet Union. Information about the Soviet Union today—religion, human rights, peace activity, etc. History of U.S.–Soviet relations. Soviet viewpoint on arms control and U.S.–Soviet relations. Glossary of terms.

Materials: Current books, pamphlets, and articles, curriculum packages, audiovisual materials, and lists of organizations that can be contacted for additional information, speakers, activities. Use of appropriate articles in newspapers and magazines is encouraged.

Instructional Methods:
1. Ten-question multiple choice quiz for students (not to be graded).
2. Answer sheet for self-grading of quiz.
3. Teachers' guide furnishes additional information about each question, as well as topics and issues for further discussion.
4. Suggestions for additional class activities and individual research topics.

Cognitive Objectives:
To present information about the Soviet Union—history, geography, present conditions, views on arms control and U.S.–Soviet relations.

To develop skills in analyzing data and in critical thinking.

To foster continuing interest in U.S.–Soviet relations as a crucial factor in maintaining world peace.

Affective Objectives:
To examine attitudes about the Soviet Union, and the basis for them.

To instill in students the knowledge that they count in the democratic process, and to impart to them the confidence they need to work for change in our society.

PURPOSE

1. To examine attitudes and ideas about the Soviet Union.
2. To identify and examine our sources of information about the Soviet Union.
3. To present information about the Soviet Union, particularly about the lives of Soviet children.
4. To examine the attitudes of Soviet children toward the possibility of war, whether nuclear or conventional.
5. To explore similarities and differences in the lives and attitudes of children in the Soviet Union and the United States.
6. To encourage continuing interest in U.S.-Soviet relations and their effect on world peace.
7. To stimulate interest in exchanges between children in the Soviet Union and the United States.
8. To motivate student participation in the democratic process.

What Some Experts Say:

For all their historical and ideological differences, these two peoples — the Russians and the Americans — complement each other; they need each other; they can enrich each other; together, granted the requisite insight and restraint, they can do more than any other two powers to assure world peace. (George F. Kennan, *Fellowship*, Jan./Feb. 84, PEP Reprint #472)

Do mainstream American newspapers, magazines, and television networks, with their collective power to shape public opinion and influence government policy, give concerned citizens a balanced view of the Soviet Union?

Whether purposely or inadvertently, they fail to do so in at least three fundamental ways. . . . Media coverage systematically highlights the negative aspects of the Soviet domestic system while obscuring the positive, . . . employs special political terms that are inherently biased, . . . [and] creates a popular perception that the Soviet Union is guilty of every charge made against it. . . .

A growing body of more balanced information about Soviet life has been available since the 1960s. It has had little positive impact on the media or on public opinion. . . . Clearly, the problem is also American indifference or resistance to balanced information about the Soviet Union. (Stephen F. Cohen, "Sovieticus," *The Nation*, 5/12/84; PEP Reprint #480)

DESCRIPTION OF ACTIVITIES

Activities I, II, and III are designed to give students the opportunity to express their thoughts and feelings about the Soviet Union, and to describe their images of the Soviet people. Then they examine and evaluate the sources of these impressions. Use your discretion about which of these three activities are most appropriate for your class.

Activity IV is a quiz designed to impart factual knowledge about the Soviet Union, the lives of Soviet children, and their attitudes toward war and peace.

ACTIVITY I

"What Do You Think About the Soviet Union?"

Step 1.   Ask children to make three columns on a sheet of paper, heading them 1, 2, and 3.

In Column 1 students write five descriptive words to express what they think about the Soviet Union, its government, and its people.

In Column 2 they do the same for their opinion about the United States.

In Column 3 students write five descriptive words to express what they think young people in the Soviet Union might think about the United States, its government, and its people.

Step 2.   Ask students to take turns in writing their words in three columns on the chalkboard. Then ask them to analyze these sets of words from the point of view of degree of friendliness or hostility. How valid are these impressions? Are they based on facts or on emotional reactions?

Step 3.   Ask students to name their sources of information about the Soviet Union. How accurate are these sources?

ACTIVITY II

"What Do You Think About the Soviet Union?"

In this activity, emphasize that the quality of the artwork is unimportant.

Step 1.   Ask students to draw scenes showing what they might see in the Soviet Union.

Step 2.   Ask students to draw scenes showing what they think Soviet children would be interested in seeing in the United States.

Step 3.   Ask the class to analyze the two sets of drawings. What images, thoughts, and feelings are expressed by each set? Is one set more friendly than the other? What are the sources of these images?

ACTIVITY III

"What Do You Think About the Soviet Union?"

Step 1.   Show the class a photograph or drawing of a tree-lined road. Tell them that this road is in the Soviet Union. Ask why they think the trees were planted next to the road. Note their responses.

Step 2.   On another day show the class a similar picture. Tell them that this road is in the United States. Ask them why they think the trees were planted next to the road. Note their responses.

Step 3.   Compare the two sets of responses. It has been found that many children will attribute militaristic motives to the Soviet Union and peaceable motives to the United States. Investigate the sources of their impressions.

ACTIVITY IV

"What Do You Know About the Soviet Union?"

This quiz can be used in several different ways:

For older students.   Distribute a copy of the quiz to each student. Emphasize that they will not be graded on their answers, that the purpose of the quiz is to find out how much they know about the Soviet Union so that they can become better informed. After they have filled in the answers, distribute a copy of the answer sheet to each student, or read the answers to them. Discuss each question as they mark their own or their classmates' papers. Encourage students to do further research on some topics. See the Teachers' Guide for additional information on topics and resources.

For younger students.   Read some of the questions to the students, and ask them whether the statements are true or false, or whether they cannot answer without further information. Use the statements as a starting point for discussion about the Soviet Union. Then follow up with some of the suggestions in the subsequent activities. See the Teachers' Guide for additional information about topics and resources.

What Do You Know About the Soviet Union?

Write T(True) or F(False) in front of the number of each question. The purpose of this quiz is for you to find out how much you know about the Soviet Union. You will not be graded. If you are not sure, try to guess the answer.

_____ 1. Russia and the Soviet Union are the same country.

_____ 2. The S.U. is about the same size as the U.S.

_____ 3. The population of the S.U. is a little more than that of the U.S.

_____ 4. School textbooks in the S.U. are printed in 52 different languages.

_____ 5. Most people in the S.U. speak Russian.

_____ 6. Soviet children attend school five days a week.

_____ 7. Many children in the Soviet Union learn English.

_____ 8. Most Soviet children belong to organizations and have after-school activities.

_____ 9. Soviet children read Russian translations of American books.

_____ 10. City children in the S.U. hardly ever go to the country.

_____ 11. Few Soviet children have television in their homes.

_____ 12. Soviet children are not allowed to go to church.

_____ 13. Soviet children enjoy many of the same sports as American children.

_____ 14. The U.S. and the S.U. had a joint space mission.

_____ 15. During World War II, over forty years ago, about 20 million Soviet people were killed.

_____ 16. Soviet people expect to go to war with the U.S.

_____ 17. In the Soviet Union the first day of school is "Peace Day."

_____ 18. During the World War II (1941–1945) the Soviet Union and the United States fought on the same side.

_____ 19. Soviet children think that their country can win a nuclear war.

_____ 20. Soviet children want to be friends with all the children of the world.

Answers to the Quiz

A. _Soviet land and people_ (#1–5)

1. False. The Russian Republic is the largest of the 15 republics in the Union of Soviet Socialist Republics, abbreviated USSR, or Soviet Union.

2. False. The S.U. is $2^{1}/_{2}$ times as large as the U.S.

3. True. The S.U. has about 270 million, the U.S. 230 million.

4. True. Over 100 different national groups live in the S.U.

5. True. Children who attend non-Russian schools begin the study of Russian in second grade. In that way all the people in the country can communicate with one another.

B. *Soviet children* (#6–13)

6. False. Children attend school Monday through Saturday.

7. True. All children begin their study of a foreign language by fourth grade or before. English is the most popular.

8. True. Most children between the ages of 9 and 14 belong to the Pioneer organization and have after-school clubs, sports, etc., either at Pioneer Palaces, in school, or in community center.

9. True. Most Soviet children are familiar with Mark Twain's Tom Sawyer and Huck Finn. Teenagers read Salinger's *Catcher in the Rye*, as well as stories and plays by John Cheever, John Updike, Tennessee Williams, Ernest Hemingway, Ursula LeGuin, etc.

10. False. Most children attend summer camps or visit relatives in the countryside. They may go hiking or camping with their family or friends during the year.

11. False. Most Soviet homes have television sets.

12. False. The practice of religion is not encouraged, but neither is it forbidden. More than 20,000 houses of worship function in the Soviet Union.

13. True. Soviet children ski, ice skate, swim, play soccer and other ball games, and hike. They also like to dance, listen to rock music, and wear jeans. Baseball and American football are not generally played.

C. *Can our two countries get along peaceably?* (#14–20)

14. True. Apollo-Soyuz joint mission in 1975.

15. True. Few families were not affected by death and destruction.

16. False. They are hopeful that war can be avoided.

17. True. In every classroom Peace Day is observed Sept. 1.

18. True. Both fought the German army of Adolf Hitler, and the U.S. sent supplies to the S.U.

19. False. They believe that no country can win a nuclear war. But their government feels it must keep up with the U.S. in arms.

20. True. Even though their governments may disagree.

An Interdepartmental Approach: Military Budgets

Claudia Zaslavsky's entry, "How Do We Spend Our Money?" provides the possibility for an interesting productive interdepartmental collaboration. Such collaboration is important to peace education for several reasons. First, peace education should be interdisciplinary. Resolution of the problems of peace and justice will require insights and knowledge from all the disciplines. Second, peace education programs could become more firmly rooted in the curriculum and have more of an effect upon schooling if more than one subject and especially if more than one teacher were involved. While the tendency in middle and secondary schools is to seek out cooperation with colleagues in the same subject areas or departments, cross-disciplinary cooperation is likely to be more productive of the kind of education we seek. Finally, work across departments is very helpful in enabling students to see the relevance of their studies to life outside the school and to their futures. This curriculum on military bugets is especially intended to do just that.

In the case of this curriculum, science might also be brought into the interdepartmental cooperation through the calculation of the consequences of the use and testing as well as the costs of nuclear weapons. Subjects dealing with values and ethics might also be involved. Public expenditures are very telling indicators of social values. For teacher background reading, *World Military and Social Expenditures* by Ruth Sivard, from World Priorities, Box 1003, Leesburg, VA 22075, is especially helpful.

Teachers interested in other curricula based on military spending might contact the Center for Peace and Conflict Studies at Wayne State University (see Resource Organizations).

SELECTION 15
How Do We Spend Our Money?

Entrant: Claudia Zaslavsky
Institution: Jane Addams Society, 1213 Race Street, Philadelphia, PA 19107
Grade Level: 7–12
Subject: Mathematics and/or social studies
Concepts: Application of mathematical analysis to current social problems; namely, the military budget and its effects on the lives of people in the United States, particularly working people and minorities.
Topics: National debt 1789 to 1988 (projected); military budget Fiscal Year 1985, and comparison with previous years; cuts in social services, particularly student loans. Mathematical topics: arithmetic operations involving large numbers; percents, estimation, graphing, handling statistics.
Materials: Current magazine and newspaper articles; local college catalogs.
Instructional Methods: Class discussion; solution of mathematics problems

by individuals and in groups; projects involving some research in college catalogs and current articles; role-playing; interviewing. Some activities are open-ended, providing for different levels of ability and interest.

Cognitive Objectives:

In Mathematics: For students to
1. Develop skill in computation with large number, mental arithmetic, estimation and approximation, computing percentages, computing averages, graphing, using statistics.
2. Set up and solve problems, given a body of statistical information.
3. Carry out research involving mathematics.
4. Gain experience in posing problems, as well as in solving them.

In Social Studies: For students to
1. Make sense out of newspaper articles.
2. Gain understanding of the federal budget and its ramifications.
3. See the relationship of government operations to their own lives.
4. Understand the effects of the budget on various groups of the population—the poor middle class, rich, women, Blacks, Hispanics, etc.

Affective Objectives: For students to
1. Understand the relevance of mathematics and social studies to real life.
2. Develop confidence in their ability to deal with real life problems.
3. Develop skills needed for independent thinking and analysis.
4. Encourage involvement in the political process.
5. Encourage cooperation and discussion in solving problems.
6. Exercise initiative in the investigation of issues.

Time Needed: Two or three class periods, and discretionary homework assignments.

PROCEDURE

Problems #1–3

1. Students read Paragraph I of the Introduction and discuss the information. Be sure they understand the terminology.
2. Students list and label the figures in the paragraph.
3. Students solve problems 1, 2, and 3. In #2, encourage mental arithmetic and the use of approximate numbers. Discuss how to set up #3.

Problems #4–7

1. Read and discuss Paragraph II of the Introduction.
2. Students list and label the figures in the paragraph.
3. Students solve problems #4–7. Encourage them to estimate the answers mentally, then check by using written computation or calculators.

Problems #8–10. You may want students to work in small groups and discuss their methods of solution.

Problems #11–13. Divide the class into three groups. Have each group solve one problem, then report to the class. They can use approximate numbers and scientific notation. Encourage the students to devise other ways to demonstrate the magnitude of military outlays and the national debt.

Projects #1–4. One or more may be assigned for homework. Allow ample time for research. For the graph in Project #2, the students may use Problem #8 as a model. Students should plan and sketch their graphs before they begin the graph to be presented to the Congressional Committee.

Conclusions. Students should understand the impact of these allocations of funds on poor people and minority groups.

INTRODUCTION

I. Early in 1984 President Reagan sent to Congress his proposed budget of $925 billion for Fiscal Year (FY) 1985 (October 1, 1984, to September 30, 1985). He asked Congress to appropriate $265 billion for military purposes. Five years before, in 1980, military expenditures were $140 billion. In the period FY 1981–1985 funds for social welfare programs—health, education, housing, etc.—were cut by $40 billion.

II. Usually the government spends more than it takes in, and it must borrow money. In his speech the President estimated that the 1985 deficit (expenses minus income) would be $180 billion. This deficit is added on to the national debt for past years. When President Reagan took office on January 20, 1981, the total national debt since 1789 was $950 billion. By the end of FY 1985 it will have increased by 86%. If spending continues at the present rate, the national debt is expected to be $2.6 trillion in December 1988.

PROBLEMS

1. Write the numerals: 265 billion; 2.6 trillion.

2. The population of the United States is about 230,000,000. How much, on the average, will every man, woman, and child contribute to 1985 military expenditures?

3. Find the percent of increase in military expenditures from 1980 to 1985.

4. Find the amount of the national debt as of 9/30/85.

5. The national debt at the end of 1988 is expected to be how many times as large as it was at the end of 1980?

6. If a debt of $2.6 trillion were to be divided evenly among all the people of the U.S., about how much would each person owe?

7. What groups of people are most affected by cuts in social services? What part of the increase in military expenditures from 1980 to 1985 would restore the $40 billion cut in social services?

8. The graph shows the number of jobs in various fields. Estimate the number of jobs in each field. For each job in guided missiles, how many jobs could be created in education? In consumer spending? In hospital and health care? What groups of people are most affected by unemployment when military spending increases?

9. Large corporations engaged in military production have received fat contracts and make lots of money. One example is Rockwell International, which has an $8.2 billion contract to manufacture 34 B-1B bombers. The cost of just five B-1B bombers would restore food stamps to a million poor families who lost them. Find the cost of this food stamp program. (The U.S. General Accounting Office stated: "Because of lack of competition and government support, defense contractors average 56% profit before taxes. Some make as much as 200% profit.")

10. Many cities are especially hard hit by cuts in funds for services. For example, from 1980 to 1984 New York City will have suffered a loss of about $143 million in federal aid to education. How many B-1B bombers would have about the same price tag?

11. If the Pentagon (what is a pentagon?) spends $265 billion in a year, how much will it spend in a day? an hour? a minute?

12. In February 1982 President Reagan said: "A trillion dollars would be a stack of one-thousand dollar bills 67 miles high." What is the height of the $1.8 trillion debt in one-thousand dollar bills? In one-dollar bills? Perhaps you can draw a cartoon to illustrate your answers?

13. If 1.8 trillion one-dollar bills were laid end to end, about how many times would they encircle the equator (25,000 miles)? Use approximate numbers in your calculations.

Answers to Problems (approximate, in most cases)

1. 265,000,000,000; 2,600,000,000,000
2. $1,200
3. 89%
4. $1.76 trillion
5. $2^3/4$
6. $11,000
7. One-third
8. [Possibilities for responses to this question can be found in Ruth Leger Sivard's annual report, *World Military and Social Expenditures*. The 1986 report is accompanied by a teachers guide. It is available from World Priorities, P.O. Box 25140, Washington, DC 20007.]
9. $1.2 billion
10. About three-fifths of a bomber
11. $726 million per day; $30 million per hour; $500,000 per minute
12. 120 miles; 120,000 miles (halfway to the moon)
13. 7,000 times

PROJECTS

1. Congress appropriated the following sums for the Guaranteed Student Loan program: $3.10 billion in 1983, $2.26 billion in 1984. Check the difference in tuition and other fees charged by some local colleges this year and last year, and compare with the cuts in funds. What groups are most affected by the cuts in funds?

2. These are the amounts spent by the Pentagon in the period 1980–1985 (*New York Times*, 2/2/84:B7):

1980 — $140 billion
1981 — $156.1 billion
1982 — $182.9 billion
1983 — $205 billion
1984 — $235 billion
1985 — $265 billion

Draw a bar graph to show the growth in military spending. Pretend that you will testify before a Congressional committee about these expenditures, and that you will present this graph in evidence. What arguments would you use, either for or against this type of spending?

3. Find a newspaper or magazine article that deals with any of the issues discussed in these problems and projects. Write a mathematics problem based on this article and ask your classmates to solve it. Better yet, interview a legislator or administrator of a social agency or institution to discuss these issues.

4. Use current data to update some of these problems.

SECTION IV
Senior High School Grades (10–12)

Ethical Reflection and Informed Action:
Neutrality and Objectivity

At the stage of adolescence, education for active citizenship is most important in the development of peacemakers. A comprehensive program of peace education assumes that such citizenship should be planetary and participatory. The sense of social responsibility nurtured in the elementary grades must now be directed at actual participation in the resolution of real social problems and issues. Students in the secondary grades need to develop the capacity to recognize such problems and identify the local, national, and global areas and instances in which they are manifest. They need, therefore, to develop the skills of analysis and synthesis and the capacities to envision and execute appropriate actions for dealing with problems.

Preparing students to form opinions, take positions, and actively pursue preferred policy options is generally accepted as a fundamental purpose of citizenship education. Global studies and peace education embrace this purpose with special reference to global issues and problems of violence and injustice. Problem solving is thus just as important in secondary school as it was in the earlier grades (see Selection 25).

It is important for teachers to be fully aware of and sensitive to student attitudes towards the issues and problems under study. Asserting attitude change as an educational goal is a delicate and controversial issue. However, the intentional pursuit of a teaching program to engender and/or develop particular attitudes is in fact necessary in peace education. But such practice is not professionally responsible when these attitudes are merely biases favoring specific interpretations of or solutions to problems. Rather it is attitudes toward problems in general that are to be intentionally affected. The attitudes sought are those frequently cited and widely accepted as educational goals, expressed in such language as competence, empowerment, efficacy, fairness, nonjudgmentalism, inquiry, open-mindedness, responsibility — in short, the attitudes of a committed and competent learner and a responsible citizen. The form of problem solving used for peace education will be most significant in the pursuit of affective (i.e., attitudinal) objectives. Perhaps the most important attitude to be engendered is objectivity in the analysis of problems, an intention to examine all available evidence and views. It is also important to impart an understanding that to be objective is not to be neutral. One can hold values that have a direct bearing on an issue and still pursue objective knowledge of the facts. Ethical reflection is as important as consideration of all evidence.

Cross-Cultural Capacity for Conflict Resolution

Cross-cultural proficiency as a capacity necessary to global peacemaking and problem solving also has an important role in secondary school peace education. Understanding of other cultures needs to contribute to peace and must be complemented by two other important capacities: communication and conflict management (Diallo & Reardon, 1981). The decline in the teaching of languages is a serious barrier to comprehensive peace education because speaking only one language limits our ability to understand and communicate with people of other cultures.

Cross-cultural understanding in itself is, indeed, an enriching element of education that has its own intrinsic value (see Selection 32). However, when applied to peace education it might also be integrally related to redressing injustices imposed on grounds of cultural differences, such as racism and the colonial domination of the so-called non-Western world. The process of redressing injustices in turn calls for communication skills (including, but not limited to, the use of other languages) and conflict resolution skills. As we seek to transcend cultural prejudice and stereotypes, we also need to be aware that just as attitude change alone is not adequate to the cause of peace, multicultural understanding alone is not adequate to the purposes of peace education. The stereotypes we seek to transcend are often related to real conflicts that may be affected by cultural differences but are not always caused by them. Peace education needs to help students sort out and fully understand these complexities in learning to diagnose problems.

An important element in the problem-diagnosis structural analyses in the study of global issues is the present international system. Imparting knowledge of the system and how it operates should be a cognitive objective of peace education (see Selection 27). Such knowledge should be pursued within the context of critical inquiry, just as knowledge of global problems is. The question of whether the present international system is capable of dealing adequately with current global problems is a fundamental aspect of world order inquiry that has long been a point of distinction between "peace studies" and "international relations," and to some degree between peace education and global education (Weston, Schwenninger, & Shamis, 1978; Reardon, 1988).

A more serious study of value conflicts and controversies, particularly those imbedded in policy questions, should certainly be introduced in the secondary grades, encouraging young people to confront issues in a more analytic manner (see Selection 26). The growing level of sophistication and the possibility of exposure to a variety of often conflicting sources of information present a special challenge to peace educators working in the ninth and tenth grades. The standard curricula also offer a special opportunity in these grades, particularly in the social studies where global issues, world cultures, and/or world history are often taught. It is in these grades that the global-perspective and world-problems orientations can be complemented by significant skills development, including values analysis, particularly those values related to the resolution of global problems.

Conflict is viewed in peace education as a normal and frequently necessary part of life. Violent conflict is generally seen as the major problem addressed by peace education. If we define of violence as unnecessary and/or avoidable harm, then peace education needs to help students to identify and explore that harm which is unnecessary and avoidable. Curricula should consider the causes of violence and alternatives for dealing with it (see Selection 17). Such inquiry is at the very heart of secondary level peace education. Study of violence at the secondary level should also include structural violence, such as poverty, racism, and the violation of human rights. Structural violence is the harm that results from social structures and systems that place some in positions of privilege and power while depriving others of fair access to the benefits of society. Peace education at the secondary level can provide students with the tools of structural analysis to enable them to understand this form of violence (see Selection 29).

Systems and Participatory Learning

One characteristic that differentiates current peace education from that of previous decades is the lack of attention to the institution of war and what is frequently termed "the war system" as well as the absence of case studies of wars that so characterized earlier peace education efforts. While American peace education in the seventies placed more emphasis on the specific case of Vietnam (a war only now coming back into the curricula) than on the institution of war, there was nonetheless more attention to war as a general problem and to international institutions as mechanisms for dispute resolution than is now the case. Nuclear education in current secondary curricula pays little attention to systems and institutions; rather it appears to focus on three major areas: the nuclear arms race, U.S./Soviet relations, and conflict resolution. Nor does it appear to emphasize global perspectives on the arms race, multilateral approaches to disarmament, the

United Nations or alternative institutions as agencies for international dispute settlement, or the concept of alternative security systems. However, some few veteran peace educators (see, for example, Ryder, Selection 28, and Scrofani, Selection 20) continue to teach well-designed units on the war system and proposals and institutions for international peacekeeping and dispute resolution.

Participatory learning is a method especially well suited to education for active global citizenship and to instruction about systems and institutions. Learning by doing has been an effective approach in the development of peace values (Laor, 1976), as has been seen in programs that include a community- or political-action component. It is also a means to achieving significant cognitive learning, especially in regard to social and political systems and processes. Simulation and games have been among the most successful teaching devices to involve learners in an actual experience of how a system or organization operates (Thorpe & Reardon, 1971). Student model UNs and various mock world conferences have been enjoyable and fruitful learning experiences for many students (see Selection 19). They have been organized locally, regionally, nationally, even internationally. They also have been used as the basis of exciting schoolwide programs much in the spirit of the infusion of global education into the entire program (see Selection 30).

Serious Lacks in the Secondary School Curricula

The imperative of nuclear literacy as an essential element of citizenship education in "the nuclear age" makes special demands on secondary science education. Yet very few survey entries came from science teachers, and none from teachers of physics, the science most important to the study of nuclear issues. Because we believe that peace education must respond to these imperatives, we sought out some suitable curricula for senior high school physics courses for inclusion in the Teachers College Peace Education Curriculum Bank. With the help of Irma Jarcho of the New Lincoln School in New York City, we reviewed material collected by the Teachers' Clearinghouse for Science and Society Education at the New Lincoln School (210 East 77th St., New York 10021). That review produced three curricula which help to fill the serious science gap in the materials garnered through the survey (for descriptions of these curricula, see "Science Education" in Recommended Curriculum Materials). The ethical issues related to the application of science form an especially important aspect of education for social responsibility that fortunately is now being given some attention in secondary level curricula (see Selection 31).

In the secondary grades, where so much emphasis is placed on rational, reflective approaches, care must also be taken to keep alive and deepen the aesthetic and celebrative capacities featured in the earlier grades (see Selections 33, 34, and 35). Far more attention needs to be devoted to developing high school peace education materials for use in language and literature, music, and all the arts. The ability to engage in cognitive processes must be complemented and integrated with the affective capacities to find meaning and to celebrate beauty and human solidarity. Such capacities are vital to exercising global responsibility for preserving the health and beauty of the planet and pursuing the unity and well-being of the human family, two overarching goals toward which all teachers and learners engaged in peace education are striving.

Special Education: Peace Education for All

Peace education is developing as a field that encompasses learners of all ages in all learning settings. Certainly in schools it should be available to all students. Physical or other conditions that prevent students from following some standard or "packaged" curriculum should not preclude their involvement in peace education. Education for empowerment as a citizen and as a person is especially important to those faced with the challenges of prejudice, stereotyping, and physical differences.

The development of self-esteem and positive attitudes toward human differences are two essential affective objectives of peace education. For the physically challenged these objectives have special significance. They need to develop a positive self-image that transcends the notion that physical differences are signs of inferiority or lesser human value. The value placed on the human dignity of all requires that students understand and respect physical challenges as they do various other human differences. This requirement and the needs noted above all are recognized in the course offered to hearing-impaired students at the Tyee High School by Regina Carter. It is offered here as an encouragement to other special education teachers to adapt appropriate aspects of peace education to the particular needs of physically challenged students.

SELECTION 16
Conflicts and Choices

Entrant: Regina Carretta
School: Tyee High School, 4424 S. 188th, Seattle, WA 98188
Grade Level: 9–12 (emphasis at 12th grade)

Subject: Senior history (for the hearing impaired)
Concepts:
    1. Conflict resolution
    2. Decision making
    3. "Personal" power to make a difference
Instructional Methods:
    Direct lecture
    Group discussion
    Interviews
    Opinion surveys
    Simulations
    Role plays
    Research
Cognitive Objectives: Students will be able to apply the alternative conflict resolution strategies to simulated conflict situations. Students will understand their rights as listed in the Bill of Rights.
Affective Objectives: Students will develop self-esteem and respect for others. Students will evaluate their own feelings about the Russian people.

BACKGROUND

The following unit has been taught for several years to twelfth-graders, in a one-semester senior history class. The population is deaf/hearing impaired. The unit is centered around the curriculum, "Choices: A Unit on Conflict and Nuclear War," published by the National Education Association [see Recommended Curriculum Materials].

TOPICS COVERED

  I. "Personal Peace"
    A. Self-esteem (define; how to increase; what affects, etc.)
    B. Decision-making skills
    C. Communication (define; how to improve; roadblocks, etc.)
    D. Conflict resolution
    E. You and your community
      1. Understanding local, state, federal governments
      2. Understanding your rights as a citizen under the Bill of Rights
 II. Personal Peace and the World Community
    A. Brainstorm—What is peace?

B. Brainstorm — What is war?
C. Brainstorm — Who are the Russians?
D. Prejudices:
   1. Explore personal prejudices
   2. Causes
   3. Reasons prejudices continue
E. Brainstorm — Alternatives for conflict resolution
F. Understanding what has come before. Suggested topics include:
   1. Hiroshima
   2. Martin Luther King
   3. The Vietnam War
G. Understanding your feelings about nuclear war (personal action, fears, hopes, etc.)
H. Understanding vocabulary related to the nuclear age (use "Choices" curriculum)
I. Investigating and understanding "Personal Power": Situations where one person has made the difference

MATERIALS/FILMS USED

Books

Self-Esteem: *Taking Charge of Your Life*, by Leland W. Howe (Allen, TX: Argus Communications, 1977).
Citizen's Rights: *Democracy in Action*, by Thomas A. Rakes & Annie DeCaprio (Austin, TX: Steck-Vaughn, 1979); *Prejudices: The Invisible Wall*, A Scope Anthology (New York: Scholastic, 1968).
"What Has Come Before": *Yesterday, Today, and Tomorrow*, by Ira Peck, Steven Jantzen, & Daniel Rosen (New York: Scholastic, 1983); *Hiroshima*, by John Hersey (New York: Knopf, 1946).
Peace Education: *The Hundredth Monkey*, by Ken Keyes (Coos Bay, OR: Living Love, 1982); *Choices: A Unit on Conflict and Nuclear War* (Massachusetts Teachers Association, 1983).

Films

Neighbors, Canadian nonverbal film about conflict
Martin Luther King
The Day After, television movie
The Deerhunter, commercial film on the Vietnam War and how it affected communities

ACTIVITIES

Interviews: Have students interview people in their community or family about their feelings on war, the arms talks, on being an armed
forces veteran; etc.
Guest Speakers: doctors, Vietnam vets, lawyers, etc.

Many other topics that come up in class are related to peace education.
The hearing-impaired population has an invisible disability, and they are
learning to deal with prejudices, inequality, and barriers to communication.
The students are learning to take this personal challenge and use it as a
means of interpreting the situations of others throughout the world who
may be exploited and struggling for peace.

Violence: The Antithesis of Peace

The entry submitted by Mary Jo Kohn, a tenth through twelfth grade
religion course, "Peace or Violence," focuses on the interrelationships among
and between different forms of violence. It also considers violence as it occurs
on all levels of human experience, from personal to global.

It is, indeed, important for secondary school students to have an opportunity to give broad and serious consideration to the various ways in which our
society is afflicted by violence. However, for the sake of balance, it is just as
important that they give equally broad and serious consideration to nonviolent
alternatives, in all their various forms and in relation to dealing with the very
instances of violence being studied. In that regard, the Bickmore curriculum
(Selection 18) would be an especially useful complement to this one. While we,
of course, advocate that all students learn about Gandhi and King, we argue
that nonviolence should not be taught as the special mission of heroes and
martyrs. It should also be demonstrated that there are many historic instances
of nonviolence in struggles against oppression and defense against aggression, and that there are examples from many parts of the world (Sharp, 1974).

There is a need for going beyond a review of types of violence in our own
society. We need to develop an inquiry into the nature and extent of violence in
the world, the interrelationships among instances of violence at various levels
of social organization, and the links between forceful violence (war and crime)
and structural violence—what this curriculum refers to as "overt" and "covert"
violence.

SELECTION 17
Peace or Violence

Entrant: Mary Jo Kohn (entry submitted by Dolores Kaczmarczyk, Assistant Principal)

School: Bishop Borgess High School, 11685 Appleton, Redford, MI 48239-1495

Grade Level: 10, 11, 12

Subject: Religion

Concepts:
  A. There is a relation between personal, community, and global violence; as there is a relation between personal, community, and global peace.
  B. There is a developmental pattern in moving from violence to peace.
  C. Human rights and dignity
  D. Social justice
  E. International understanding and cooperation
  F. Nonviolent approaches to conflict
  G. The Gospel approach to relationships

Topics:

  A. Aggression, assertiveness
  B. Violence in media
  C. Violence in sports
  D. Suicide
  E. Family violence
  F. Street violence
  G. Criminal justice system and prisons
  I. Peace and the Gospel
  J. Nonviolent approaches to violence
  K. Civil disobedience and conscientious objection
  L. Nuclear arms race
  M. Global terrorism

Instructional Methods: Media, lecture, discussion, home experiments, role-playing, simulation games, book reviews.

Cognitive Objectives:
  A. That students know the research and debate about overt and covert violence in each topical area
  B. That students are able to know and use the definitions of the language of violence, peace, justice, etc.
  C. That students know the solutions that individuals and society have proposed and try to implement them
  D. That students examine the adequacies of these solutions
  E. That they examine other solutions
  F. That they are able to apply the teaching of the Gospel to the solutions

Affective Objectives:
    A. That the students examine their own aggression and assertiveness and consider directions for the future
    B. That students' consciousness be raised in the areas of violence and peacemaking
    C. That students recognize the relationships between different forms of violence
    D. That students examine their own values
    E. That students use the information to form a conscience for the future

OVERVIEW

The basic rationale of this course is to give the students a chance to study and analyze violence in our society and form a Christian conscience towards it. Christ challenges us to live as peacemakers in a violent world. This course focuses on specific areas of violence in our lives and searches for peaceful alternatives of response.

    I. Aggression, Non-assertiveness, and Assertiveness
       A. Man's aggressive impulse
       B. Other ways of dealing with aggressive feelings
   II. Violence in Media
       A. Impact of media
       B. Violence in TV
       C. Violence in other media
       D. Media violence analysis project
  III. Violence in Sports
       A. Sports as acceptable expression of aggression: an American "religion"
       B. Sports and physical violence
       C. Sports and prejudice (covert violence)
       D. Sports and the psyche
          1. College athletics
          2. Winning and losing: Does the end justify the means?
          3. Coaching
          4. Little League
       E. The fans
       F. The new coliseum
  IV. Suicide
       A. Suicide rates in modern life
       B. Danger signals
       C. Dealing with a crisis

D. Prevention
E. Suicide and teens
V. Family Violence
  A. Child Abuse
    1. Definitions and history
    2. Who is the abuser?
    3. Cycle of violence in the family
    4. Detection and responsibilities of the community
    5. Attempted treatment and problems of community involvement
  B. Spouse Abuse
    1. Who is the abuser?
    2. Who is the victim?
    3. Why do they stay?
    4. Response of the community and the law
    5. Attempted solutions
VI. Violence in the Streets
  A. Victims and the prejudices of society
  B. Rape
  C. Murder
  D. Self-defense
  E. Gun control
VIII. Violence in the Criminal Justice System
  A. The rights of the accused: Violence in court
  B. Violence in prisons
IX. War
  A. Using resources for destruction
  B. The Holocaust ("Night and Fog," a film by Alain Resnais)
  C. Effects on civilians
  D. Effects on soldiers and the meaning of aggression in action
X. Peace
  A. Peace and the Gospel
  B. Civil disobedience vs. violent dissent
  C. Peacemakers: Gandhi and King
  D. Conscientious objection
XI. The Arms Race and Nuclear Power
  A. Arms producers and salesmen
  B. Weaponry
  C. Nuclear production and dangers
  D. Proposals for disarmament
  E. The military industrial complex and arms
  F. Relationship between arms production and hunger, poverty, etc.
XII. Terrorism and the Global Community

Alternatives to Violence: The Foundations of Peace

As a problem-solving discipline, peace education requires both a diagnostic component (see Selection 17) and a prescriptive one. The search for alternatives to violence, the major prescriptive inquiry of peace studies, should occupy a major place in the curricula of peace education. The Alternatives to Violence Education Project has developed and published an excellent, comprehensive, creatively conceived syllabus in the form of "A Manual for Teaching Peacemaking to Youth and Adults."

The manual written by Kathy Bickmore provides directions and curricula for workshop facilitation and serves as an introductory course for Grades 10–12. It is highly recommended as a standard course and "required reading" for peace educators. For those who are unable to obtain the manual itself, descriptions of three instructional games are excerpted here.

As exemplars of lesson plans for teaching prescriptive skills we have selected three sessions from the manual that deal with prescribing alternatives to violence at the global and the personal levels. Session 13 has been selected primarily because it can be used as a culminating exercise for several important peace education topics and methods. Session 14 could be used to teach the concept of alternative security systems and defense policies. Session 19, a disciplined exercise in creative imagination, will be helpful to peace educators who want to emphasize disarmament education and alternatives to war (see *Peace Research Reviews, 9*(1), on the abolition of war). It is an especially useful example of the imaging process advocated in this guide (see Selections 5 and 6).

SELECTION 18
Alternatives to Violence

Entrant: Kathy Bickmore and the Northeast Ohio Alternatives to Violence Committee

Institution: Alternatives to Violence Education Project, 10916 Magnolia Drive, Cleveland, OH 44106

Grade Level: Written for high school (9–12); has been used in Grades 7 and 8 and with adults.

Subject: Social studies and language arts (English), occasionally extracurricular

Concepts: Nonviolence is more than the absence of violence: It involves many different possible tactics for confronting and resolving conflict. Some of these tactics require verbal skills; others do not. An improved understanding of the relationships between the types of violence and nonviolence in our lives and the conflicts which cause them allows us to make our own decisions more effectively. Nonviolence can be uniquely effective — even fun.

Topics: The theory, history (case studies), and practice of nonviolent action: Personal conflict resolution, including listening/expressing, negotiating, leading/facilitating, and self-defense. Community conflict resolution, including causes of conflict and violence in our communities and responses to institutional violence and injustice. Global conflict resolution, including roots of war, nonviolent national defense, how to write a letter to Congressional representatives, and imaging a world without weapons.

Materials and/or Media: [The published edition from which this selection is extracted includes a bibliography that is not reproduced here; contact the Project for more information.] Audio-visual options include: "Hiroshima-Nagasaki: 1945," "Neighbors," "Guess Who's Coming to Breakfast," "Choice or Chance," "Active Non-violence," and "The Big IF."

Instructional Methods: Participatory, often fun, meant to develop leadership: discussion, role-playing, games of many kinds (some with a specific "lesson," others for affirmation and community-building), analysis of case studies, journal writing, and imaging. Lots of change between types of activities, small- or large-group work, facilitators, etc. Participants are encouraged to lead when they wish, voice skepticism when they feel it, affirm their own actions and needs and those of others in the group, and so on.

Cognitive Objectives: (1) To generate an awareness of the many creative nonviolent actions that have been used and can be used. (2) To expand students' understanding of violence by considering sources as well as symptoms. Particularly, to understand better basic human needs and how they may be met, or how people act when they perceive that needs are not being met. (3) To develop personal conflict resolution skills, such as listening, expressing needs, negotiating, writing, peacemaking, and maintaining personal safety, and to forge a relationship between understanding these skills and the larger scale.

Affective Objectives: While there certainly often are value-oriented or attitudinal changes in many of the students who go through the Alternatives to Violence course, it is more the awareness than the attitudinal change that is the ATV leader's goal. Possibly the attitudinal change that we most encourage is the improvement of the participants' self-esteem, particularly the sense of one's own power to affect the environment and make positive changes when and where one desires. As the students increase their understanding of what causes violence and what causes/encourages nonviolence, as well as increasing their awareness of the effectiveness of nonviolence in their own lives, we are pleased when they sometimes cease to feel that violence is inevitable.

SESSION 13
ALTERNATIVES TO VIOLENCE ON THE GLOBAL LEVEL

Goals: To apply concepts and skills for interpersonal and community conflict resolution to global problems.

Materials:

"Guess Who's Coming to Breakfast" slideshow
slide projector
cassette tape player
screen
chart model (on board or easel)

Plan:

A. Show "Guess Who's Coming to Breakfast" (20 mins.). NOTE: You may wish to substitute another slideshow, "Sharing Global Resources," with older groups if you wish. It is longer, however, and this will severely limit discussion time.

B. Discussion (10–15 mins.). Here are some questions to ask:
How do you feel about belonging to a "global family"?
What is "global responsibility"?
Consider the relationship of the individual to the world, particularly beyond national boundaries.
What does it mean to be a world citizen?
Should individuals like us become involved in world affairs?
In what ways? Why?

C. Discuss the chart, "Conflict Resolution on Three Levels" (see Chart 18.1) (5–10 mins.). Ask people to share with the groups ways in which they may have exercised global responsibility through travel, study, boycotts, and so forth. Fill in the chart with these examples.

D. Make assignments for the next session:
  1. Reading
  2. Suggested questions to address in journal: What role do I (or can I) have in confronting violence at the global level?

Chart 18.1: Conflict Resolution on Three Levels

PERSONAL	COMMUNITY	GLOBAL

ACTIVE LISTENING
 	
FACT FINDING
	Hearings
	Research
	Investigative reporting
	Discussion of community
	   issues with various people
	Awareness of local news
		Travel
		Study of other cultures
		International organizations
		Investigative reporting
		Awareness of international
		   news (via TV, radio, news-
		   papers, and so on)

LEADING FACILITATING	Legislation Community organizing efforts Executive action Personal witness Education	Government leadership United Nations Disarmament movements Research to develop appropriate technology

NEGOTIATING	Use of the courts
	Legislative hearings
	   and debates
	Union–Management negotiation
	Town, school, and
	   neighborhood meetings
	Community mediation centers
		Diplomacy
		World court
		Trade agreements
		International non–govern-
		   mental organization
		U.N. Special Sessions and
		   General Assembly meetings

PRACTICING ACTIVE
   NONVIOLENCE
	Letters to government
	   representatives
	Lobbying
	Public speaking
	Demonstrations
	Voting
	Relief work
	Boycotts
	Strikes
	Political campaigns
	Civil disobedience
	"Alternative to violence:"
	   teaching, learning, and
	   practicing
		U.N. campaigns (for the
		   New International Economic
		   Order [NIEO], disarmament,
		   and so on)
		Boycotts of goods, trade,
		   or services
		Trade embargoes
		Relief work
		Nonviolent civilian
		   national defense

Leader draws the chart on the board and fills in the major headings (words in capital letters);
group members brainstorm to fill in the right-hand spaces (words in lower case letters are
examples which the leader can use to supplement the group's ideas).

SESSION 14
NONVIOLENT NATIONAL DEFENSE

Goals:

1. To address honestly our personal attitudes toward national security
2. To explore creative methods of nonviolent civilian national defense

Materials.   World map

Reading due.   Case #14, A–F; "Disregarded History" (G. Sharp)

Plan:

A. Map exercise (5–10 mins.). Have group members point out the major "hot spots" around the world (i.e., places where wars are taking place or conflicts could easily develop into wars). Ask what is happening in each place, and why.

B. Pick one "hot spot" with which most group members are familiar, develop together a fairly detailed scenario showing how the conflict or war began and developed (10 mins.).

Discuss how wars generally begin and what causes wars. Then ask: Has nuclear weapons technology changed the ways wars happen or could happen?

C. Define nonviolent national defense: Nonviolent defense entails total, collective, noncooperation with the attacking force (20–25 mins.).

Examples include striking (a general strike would mean everyone would refuse to work; this would, in effect, shut down the country or area); boycotting goods or services or meetings of the attacking or the occupying groups; closing down communication systems, power systems, and so forth; removing street signs to make it more difficult to arrest dissenters. . . . Discuss (in smaller working groups if people wish) the concept of national security, using these questions:

What makes us feel more secure? Less secure?

What would we need to learn and do in order to move closer to a more secure United States?

How do you feel about the disarmament movement?

How do you feel about U.S. weapons sales to other countries?

How do you feel about the amount of money the U.S. government spends for the military vs. other programs?

D. How do you feel about the "Soviet Threat"? What can we do as individuals and as a nation to lessen the tension between the U.S. and the U.S.S.R.?

SESSION 19
IMAGING A WORLD WITHOUT WEAPONS

Goals:

1. To imagine how our world would look without weapons
2. To discuss what steps each of us could take to help move the world away from violence

Materials:

> Chart on board or easel, chalk or markers and paper
> List of local and national groups working on peaceful change
> Lists of other resources

Reading due.   Review course readings.

Plan:

A. Imaging a world without weapons (20–25 mins.). Introduction:

> This session is based on a much longer workshop, "Imaging a World Without Weapons," developed by Elise Boulding and Warren Ziegler and others. What we will do today is just a small taste of what could happen in a longer session.
>
> We are going to transport ourselves in an imaginary time machine into a quite different world: thirty years in the future, in a world where violence exists, but people have made a conscious decision to abolish weapons. It is important that we really "live" in this world — we speak in the present tense ("it is," rather than "it will be/should be"), not as if we are planning the future.

Encourage people to really let their imaginations go — describe a world they really want to live in. After giving the group a minute or two to think (and possibly take notes for themselves), ask members to describe, in brief phrases, highlights of what they see (imagine) before them. Write all these phrases on the board. NOTE: It is helpful to ask participants to close their eyes at first.

B. Have the group members become "historians" who are living in the year 2014 (10 mins.). [Begin by drawing a chart that has three columns, each headed by a span of years. The first column (the imagined present) should be labeled 2000–2014; the second, 1990–2000; and the third, 1984–1990.] Introduce the exercise:

> Now we become "historians." Let's look back over the last forty years and recall what has happened at various stages to bring us to this point — to a world without weapons. For each period on this chart, we will brainstorm and fill in the column. Let's begin with the last few years, 2000–2014.

Repeat the brainstorming for each of the other periods, for example, 1990–2000 and 1984–1990. As the brainstorming proceeds, people will begin to see causal relationships among events and begin to move them to different columns to reflect the order in which they would have to happen.

C. Have group members discuss their feelings about the "imaging" exercise (5-10 mins.). Give out the list of resources and action groups. Ask participants to share with the group their plans/ideas for continuing to learn and work for peace and justice — specific actions, organizations, and so forth.

Optional. If more time is available for Section A, have participants divide into small groups with particular focuses: education, recreation/family life, governance/conflict resolution, defense/security systems, transportation/communication, and so forth. Each group then describes in more detail the way the world looks in its particular field and reports back to the whole group at the end of the exercise.

Simulating a System: The United Nations

"World Assembly: A Mock United Nations," by Janet Chaniot and Marge Gericke of the Potter Valley Schools, invites students into a participatory experience that enables them to learn about global problems while simulating a United Nations General Assembly. This curriculum is multi-grade level, participatory, and focuses on the United Nations. Few global studies and peace education programs give adequate attention to the world organization. A thorough knowledge of the UN is as important to preparation for global citizenship as knowledge of national political culture and structures is to preparation for national citizenship. There are possibilities for study of the UN at every grade level. It is recommended that teachers contact the organization for information on the materials and programs it offers for all ages (see Resource Organizations).

The United Nations is the most appropriate vehicle through which to provide a global perspective on world issues. Its efforts and publications treat virtually every global problem (see *World Concerns and the UN*, Recommended Curriculum Materials). Its highly significant efforts on behalf of positive peace are generally ignored by global education. Its various worldwide efforts dealing with the problems of education, environment, development, poverty, hunger, health, and human rights are rarely reflected in curriculum materials. Even most of those who sent in responses to the peace education curriculum survey viewed the UN only from the perspective of conflict and peacekeeping (see, for example, Selection 20). The following curriculum is a notable and useful exception.

SELECTION 19
World Assembly: A Mock United Nations

Entrant: Janet Chaniot and Marge Gericke
School: Potter Valley Schools, Box 219, Potter Valley, CA 95469
Grade Level: At our school the World Assembly has involved students in grades 5-12.
Department: Although the World Assembly has been primarily an English/ social science project, it is becoming interdisciplinary.
Concepts:
    A. Global interdependence is a fact of life.
    B. Recognition of everyone's basic needs and human rights is necessary for survival on our planet.
    C. People must work together at every level (local, state, national, regional, and global) to increase communication skills, understanding, and our ability to use Earth's resources for peaceful living.
Topics:
    A. Geography (physical, cultural, and economic) of nations selected each year to be represented in the World Assembly
    B. Current issues, such as world hunger, desertification, war, nuclear energy, and refugees
    C. The United Nations' organization and agencies: evolving processes to achieve peace.
Instructional Methods:
    A. Deductive: testing concepts by gathering information
    B. Inductive: seeing patterns and forming concepts from information
    C. Large Group: lectures, reports, note-taking, rehearsal of World Assembly pageant and debates
    D. Small Group: map making, flag making, library study of teacher-made study guides on countries and current issues
    E. Individual: reading assignments, letter writing, phone calls
Cognitive Objectives: Using Bloom's "taxonomy of critical thinking,"[1] we see the learning objectives as follows: *literal*—learning about countries, regions, and issues; *inferential*—drawing conclusions and forming resolutions from study materials; *application*—discussing materials in groups, seeing local implications of global issues, selecting resolutions for debate; *analysis*—debating the issues and resolutions; *synthesis*—

---

[1]Benjamin S. Bloom, ed., *Taxonomy of Educational Objectives* (New York: David McKay, 1956).

participating in the World Assembly and sending results to government
officials and the United Nations.

Affective Objectives: Affective learning centered on the philosophical concepts of ourselves and our classes as microcosms of the larger world
and of our ability to influence the direction of history in our community and the world.

   A. Seeking to understand Maslow's "hierarchy of needs"[2] — food, water,
      shelter, clothing, love and respect, self-actualization, and success.

   B. Discovering through the "magic circle of sharing and caring" that
      "we can lead or help others if we first know ourselves."

   C. Learning about setting limits — How can we lead others if we have
      no self-discipline?

SUGGESTED SCHEDULE

First Month

   Elect officers
   Select countries or regions
   Choose committees (correspondence, set-up, clean-up, music, displays)
   Begin collecting resources
   Prepare study questions and lists of issues

Second Month

   Prepare master sheets and resolutions
   Begin rehearsal in class and with other classes
   Invite guests

Third Month

   Rehearse and perform World Assembly
   Publish materials and results in local news media
   Send materials and results to public officials and the United Nations
   Evaluate the program and plan for next year

---

[2]Abraham Maslow, *Toward a Psychology of Being*, 2nd ed. (New York: Van Nostrand,
1968).

SUGGESTED MATERIALS FOR A MODEL UNITED NATIONS

NOTE: The following materials are ones that we have found most useful in creating a World Assembly each year. There are certainly more materials available; seek out and select those most suited to the local situation and its perspective on global issues.

Periodicals

>*Junior Scholastic* and other Scholastic publications
>*Christian Science Monitor*
>New York *Times*
>San Francisco *Chronicle*
>*National Geographic*
>*Newsweek*
>*Time*
>*World Press Review*

For Reference

>*The World Almanac*
>Ferguson, *The Aquarian Conspiracy*
>Mehlinger, et al., *Global Studies* (National Education Association)
>Naisbett, *Megatrends*
>Schell, *The Fate of the Earth*
>Publications of the United Nations

Activities

>Reviewing research skills
>Checking available resources
>Taking notes
>Summarizing
>Writing letters to consuls, public officials, pen pals
>Writing articles and notes for publication
>Designing programs and posters
>Preparing information on issues and countries, resolutions to present in the World Assembly, and dialogues on the issues
>Practicing debate skills
>Making maps, flags, ethnic music tapes, cartoons, collages
>Electing Assembly officials
>Sampling international foods

Rehearsing parts for the model UN performance
Performing the World Assembly Pageant

WORLD ASSEMBLY STUDY GUIDE

Directions: Answer all questions in complete sentences. Do three resolutions according to the example. Write your dialogue after you have seen the sample dialogue (provided by teacher).

Factual Information

1. What is the location of your country?
2. What are the major cities?
3. What is the population?
4. What are the major ecosystems?
5. What is the Gross National Product (GNP)?
6. What is the average annual wage?
7. Name the major landforms: mountains, deserts, etc.
8. Name the major bodies of water.
9. Who are the current leaders?
10. What type of government exists in your country?
11. Name your country's resources.
12. Name the major products of your country.
13. What tourist attractions exist in your country?
14. What makes people proud to live in your country?
15. Which of your citizens (past or present) do people admire? What achievements are they admired for?
16. What are the major problems your country faces?
17. How can your country help another country solve its problems?
18. What would your country expect from that country in exchange?
19. Describe the lifestyle of the "average" citizen of your country.
20. What do you find particularly interesting about your country?

Resolutions

Write at least three resolutions, on any of the suggested issues, that could be debated in the World Assembly.

Example: Resolved: that the countries in the World Assembly devote 2% of their GNP to solving the problem of hunger in the world.

Issues: Pollution, desertification, nuclear arms, war (conventional or nuclear), hunger, health, populations, immigration, refugees, peace, use of resources, use of products, use of technology, use of political, social or economic advisers.

Dialogue

Write a dialogue among several countries for one of your resolutions.

Conflict: The Study of War in a District-wide K–12 Program

The curriculum of E. Robert Scrofani of the Berkeley High School History Department, "Peace and War, a Unit on Conflict," combines an alternative to war with a nuclear education approach. A description of the development of the program introduces the curriculum. Especially useful to school administrators and groups of faculty wishing to undertake peace education is the process of formulating fundamental purposes, defining the basic concepts, establishing the learning goals for the program, and projecting a curriculum to meet the goals that fully integrates the purposes and the concepts. Such a holistic approach to curriculum development is well suited to a comprehensive sequential peace education program. Indeed, it is appropriate to all curriculum planning.

The curriculum excerpts constitute only a course outline, so teachers will have to develop their own specific instructional methods. As an example of one possible technique to use, see Selection 21. This excerpt outlines a model-building method that can be used to complement the imaging techniques suggested by Bickmore (Selection 18).

The course outline that appears here is the secondary level component of a K–12 course and unit-based district-wide peace education program.

SELECTION 20
Peace and War

Entrant: E. Robert Scrofani
School: Berkeley High School, 2246 Milvia Avenue, Berkeley, CA 94704
Grade: 9–12
Department: Social Science/History
Concepts: Conflict, aggression, peacekeeping models, alternatives to war

Topics: Aggression, conflict, reasons for aggression; causes of war, consequences of war, responsibility for war, peacekeeping
Materials: Noted as they are used in the curriculum.
Cognitive Objectives:
  Knowledge of theories of aggression and causes of war
  Knowledge of nature of conflict and consequences of war
  Knowledge of alternatives to war and systems and proposals for international peacekeeping.
Affective Objectives:
  Appreciation of variety of possibilities for conflict resolution and peacekeeping
  Inclination to consider multiple alternatives in approaching problems and conflicts

OVERVIEW

What we did. The Berkeley High School History Department has already:

1. Held department meetings on the peace curriculum
2. Held a full-day workshop at the Teachers Center with representatives of staff of Main and East Campus with participation of two consultant-volunteers
3. Held a pre/post discussion meeting on *The Day After*
4. Showed *What About the Russians* to 15 sections
5. In 13 sections, conducted a poll on views with reference to the threat of war after the Korean airline crisis
6. Showed *The Age of the Megaton* in six sections
7. Showed *No Frames, No Boundaries* in five sections
8. Held discussions in many sections on current events regarding the nuclear problem
9. Discussed, in Model Congress classes, student proposals for legislation on the nuclear freeze and on other nuclear issues
10. Developed a series of concepts in preliminary discussion

What we are. Our groups include the members of the History Department of Berkeley High School (22) who participated in one or more discussions on the curriculum; the history staff from East Campus (2); Jean Wilkinson, a former teacher and district consultant; Nancy Rubin, high school Social Living teacher, who met with the department to discuss impact of the ABC film, *The Day After.*

What peace is.   Ten members of the staff met in an all-day session to discuss "What Peace Is . . ." Some thoughts were:

1. Life without violence; a period of self-restrained freedom
2. Life with justice for all; constructive action resulting in positive results
3. A process of accepting differences
4. Actively seeking a world without war
5. The way to a goal of meeting needs while respecting rights of others
6. Willing cooperation for justice
7. Collective social harmony

GENERAL CONSENSUS: Peace is an active process to seek justice. It is a voluntary choice to respect life by resolving conflict without resorting to violence.

What we want in our classrooms (teacher responses).   In my classroom, I want:

1. Peaceful resolution of conflict to be a stranger no longer
2. Stories about people who seek justice in society
3. Information on how various cultures at various times arrive peacefully at solutions to conflict
4. Examples of peaceful alternatives in history
5. Knowledge of what it means to be in a participatory democracy, of how to empower the people
6. The encouragement of individual responsibility
7. Knowledge of the difference between life in the Nuclear Age and in pre-nuclear times
8. Knowledge of the nature of aggression and the nature of human beings
9. An increase of critical-thinking skills
10. Knowledge of the forms of positive conflict
11. Awareness of the disparity between our ideals and our actions
12. Awareness of cultural differences in responding to conflict
13. Observation of how we respond to problems in our school community
14. Understanding of various options by which we deal with our aggression as a person and as human beings in a nation and in our world

Strategies to promote a peace curriculum. We need to provide a framework for these discussions in our classrooms. Just as teachers have differing views, students' views differ. These must be respected and be presented fairly in the classroom setting. Consensus may often be reached. Once the proper framework is established, perhaps peace can become a voluntary choice in more of our lives. There are two major strategies that can be pursued:

1. Incorporate peace discussions, activities, etc., into their proper context as we study human beings in history. Peace issues can be infused into the curriculum at various locations, or peace issues can be raised by changing emphases in areas of the curriculum.
2. Focus on conflict resolution as a theme and extend the time devoted to it.

OUTLINE

I. *First Week*: Introduction to Conflict and Aggression
   1. Define verbal, physical, and passive response to aggression.
   2. Use survey form "How Aggressive Are You?" Students should react verbally and/or in writing to the results. (Sample topic: How Aggression or Violence Affects My Life.)
      a. Students role-play a confrontation in their personal lives or in school life.
      b. Reading on aggression of a young and of an old person in "Afternoon in the Jungle" from the *New Yorker* to examine motives.
      c. Discussion leading to personal limits for aggression.
      d. Students write about real conflict situations. (Examples: brother and brother; brother and sister; "A student from our school threatens and extorts money from classmates. He is caught.") Discuss or role-play; consider appropriate punishment, etc.
II. *Second Week*: Aggression—Learned or Instinctive? (If humans are naturally aggressive, then they must provide for outlets for their aggression; if aggression is learned, they should clarify these values and deal with their consequences.)
   1. *Day 1*: Introduce readings or newspapers and magazine articles. Do a class collage based on the question/discussion. (Example: "Kill the umpire while you're at it.")
   2. *Day 2 (or 2, 3, 4)*: Show the film *Lord of the Flies*. Discussion/Questions from "Three Films and World Peace."
   3. *Day 3*: Reading from AEP Booklet *Organization Among Nations*, "Harmony and Friction at Robbers' Cave," pp. 55–60.

4. *Day 4*: Excerpts from *African Genesis* by Robert Ardrey, *Territorial Imperative* by Robert Ardrey, *On Aggression* by Konrad Lorenz.
5. *Day 5*: Panel Discussion: Is Aggression Natural or a Learned Response?

III. *Third Week*: What Are Some Causes of War?
   1. Gather from class a list of what could cause war. List could include:
      a. Propaganda (example: Cuba vs. U.S.; U.S. vs. Cuba)
      b. Weapons/weapons development
      c. Too few resources
      d. Too many people
      e. Desire for land
      f. Public attitudes
   2. Introduce the above with "Attitude Survey on Peace/War." Administer the survey both before and after the discussion.
   3. Film (or readings from): *All Quiet on the Western Front*.
   4. Current material on hunger, oil, Israeli-Arab conflict, Irish Protestant-Catholic disputes—all are appropriate to set the stage.
   5. For more accomplished students, reading/excerpts from Clauswitz, the predominant Western theorist on war, would be appropriate.

IV. *Fourth Week*: Technology and War
   1. Film: *Hiroshima and Nagasaki* demonstrates the devastation of new technology.
   2. Filmstrip: *The Age of Megaton* shows the growth of technology since 1945.
   3. Film: *Fail Safe* indicates the problems of a peace guaranteed by terror. *Fail Safe* particularly lends itself to discussion of effect of values and decisions, the effect of lack of trust, the effect of suspicion.
   4. Questions such as "If you were on the last plane heading for the U.S.S.R. and you knew the U.S.A. had been destroyed, would you continue to move toward the U.S.S.R. and drop your bomb?" can lead to revealing discussion of the role of revenge as a key value.
   5. Simulations: "A Prisoner's Dilemma" is appropriate here to indicate impact of trust. Use one or two periods for game and debriefing. "The Oil Island Dispute" is based on "A Prisoner's Dilemma."

V. *Fifth Week*: Alternatives for Conflict Resolution and Peacekeeping
   1. Film: *High Noon*—Discussion/questions
   2. Film: *The Hat*
   3. Historical attempts: AEP booklet *Organization Among Nations*, "The Concert That Brought a Century of Peace," pp. 7–9, or *Our Widening World*, by Ethel E. Ewing (Rand/McNally, 1967), pp. 492–498.
      a. Truce of God (Middle Ages)

b. Balance of Power—Post 1815

c. Detente with China/Russia

d. Pax Romana, Britannica

e. Disarmament—Post WWI

f. League of Nations

g. SALT Talks

h. UN and UN Peacekeeping Forces (in the Congo, Middle East, Cyprus)

i. Regional Pacts—NATO, SEATO, etc.

Every school text or supplementary material has something on each of the above topics. Teacher may assign several reports, then have students cooperatively share the results of their research. One way would be as follows: (1) two days of research and homework, (2) table talks, sharing information in groups of four on four different peace approaches, (3) class summary.

4. Simulation: Conflict games (requires 3–5 weeks)

VI. *Sixth Week*: The Moral Issues (Limiting war; personal responsibility)[1]

1. Film: *War* (presents idea that individual soldier holds responsibility)

2. Film: *Judgment at Nuremberg*

3. Reading: *The Flying Machine* by Ray Bradbury (presents in a delightful story the idea that scientists must be responsible for their creations)

4. Research Project (or follow-up assignments)

A Workshop on Decision Making: The Foreign Policy of the United States

Decision making (Hiroshima, Cuban Missile Crisis, U.S. Entrance into WWI, Embargo of 1807, Lend-Lease to England before WWII, Detente with Russia or China, etc.). Student should be able to isolate:

a. Situation, including the objective and subjective basis of the conflict

b. Target (goal)

c. Alternatives available

d. Consequences of alternatives

This unit not only combines values and research skills but includes also the frame of reference prior to decisions.

5. Administer the attitude survey again and analyze the results. (Particularly check the correspondence or lack of it between items.)

6. Evaluate unit.

---

[1]"War Criminals War Victims," a booklet for Grades 10–12, deals with individual responsibility in war. It is available from COPRED (see Resource Organizations)—Ed.

Testing Peacekeeping Models

The following model-building activity, extracted from *Peacekeeping* (Fraenkel, Carter, & Reardon, 1973, pp. 87–90; see World Order Series in Recommended Curriculum Materials) is suggested by the editor as a culminating exercise for curricula similar to "Peace and War" and those using futures imaging techniques. Although it is not a selection drawn from the survey, it has been frequently used in many classrooms and offers an important peace education teaching approach not represented in the survey. It is written for student readers.

SELECTION 21
Peacekeeping Models

Authors: J. Fraenkel, M. Carter, and B. Reardon
Source: Excerpted from *Peacekeeping* (New York: Random House, 1973).
    Copyright © 1973 by World Policy Institute; reproduced by permission. (Available from COPRED; see Resource Organizations.)

TESTING THE MODELS

Here is an activity to help you imagine the future. It is a kind of experiment or test of the models [i.e., (1) The League of Nations, (2) The United Nations, (3) The Cold War or Bipolar System, and (4) World Law (a proposed revision of the United Nations) — Ed.] to help you see if you prefer one, or indeed any, of the models of peacekeeping systems you have studied. By following the procedures outlined below, you should be able to compare the possible effectiveness of the four models.

1. Begin by reading the first scenario in this book, April 1, 1990. . . . Make some notes on the factors that make the situation a potential crisis for the peacekeeping system. [Teachers may use any actual or hypothetical case they feel to be appropriate to the course of study — Ed.]
2. The class should be divided into four groups of students. Each group will then select (perhaps by drawing lots) one of the four models. As a group, review the description of your model. During the discussion, keep the diagram of the system visible if you feel it might help. Be sure you remember all the parts and understand how they operate.
3. Members of those groups that chose models Nos. 1, 2, and 4 should consider themselves to be members of the Council of the international

organization suggested by their model. Members of the group testing model No. 3 should consider themselves to be advisers to the President of the United States.

4. Each group should then apply its model to the scenario (i.e., case describing events related to an international conflict). Within the limitations imposed by the model, the members should explain how they would "resolve" the crisis. In other words, they are to make recommendations about what can be done to keep the peace by using the powers and processes described in the model.

5. After considerable discussion (at least one class period), the small groups should report their suggestions to the entire class. In their reports they should include answers to the following questions:

Why did you make these recommendations?

What characteristics of your model influenced your decision?

What is it about the model that gives it strength in keeping the peace?

What characteristic(s) makes it weak in its job of peacekeeping?

6. When each of the four groups has reported, the whole class should consider which of these models was most effective in dealing with the hypothetical future crisis and why.

BUILDING YOUR OWN MODEL

Even after all this testing and rating, you and some of your classmates might not be able to choose any of the four models in this book as your preferred world. Why not build your own model? You could plan a system that might be even better than any of those you have studied. After you have completed your plan, try to present it so that everyone will understand it. Your diagram could be in the form of a very large chart that you could put on the bulletin board. How do the components of your model operate to perform the function of peacekeeping?

As you plan your model, remember to keep in mind what you think is most likely to cause war now and in the future. Then you must decide what kinds of institutions could prevent war. Plan parts for your model that could carry out the necessary preventive functions. When you present your diagram to the class, also tell them what your theory is.

TESTING YOUR OWN MODEL

While the system-designers are planning their model, another group might prepare some possible crises that could be used to test the model. This group would be a team of scenario writers. They would also have to list what might be some of the potential causes of war. This list of causes could then serve as the basis for a scenario, or group of scenarios. These scenarios could be used to try out the new model presented by the teacher. After you have made your action decisions working within your own model, raise the same questions as were raised about the other models. How did you do as peacekeepers? Do you think your plan might work?

If you really think your own plan or any of those you have studied could provide adequate security for the world community, how do you think it could be adopted? You should begin to think about how the world community might move toward whatever preferred world you have agreed upon. This is far from the end of the inquiry into peacekeeping problems and possibilities. For even after the majority of the people of the world have adopted the peace system which you prefer, the policies and actions needed to bring the plan into being have to be agreed upon.

This is a whole new area of inquiry for you to follow. And because this inquiry is a continuing one, some questions should be asked whenever you come across a plan for peacekeeping in the future.

Will this plan work?
Do we need the institutions proposed by this plan?
Is this plan fair to all who will be affected by it?
What effect might this plan for peacekeeping have on the quality of life and other global problems?
Can it provide the basis for just and lasting world peace?

And finally, there are two questions you should always ask yourself: Can the institution of war be eliminated? Can I do anything to help?

Conflict: Multiple Approaches

The concepts of alternatives to violence and multiple alternatives are well integrated in the curriculum of John Raby, first developed for the Governor's School of New Jersey. The Governor's School is particularly oriented to achieving the goals of peace education and to focusing on individual responsibility to confront global problems. It was founded by two outstanding American peace educators, Drs. Cheryl and James Keen, and is offered to high school juniors as a residential summer program.

Another fundamental peace education concept central to this curriculum is the normality of conflict. Raby aims to demonstrate that conflict does exist at all levels of human experience and that there are multiple ways for institutions and individuals to respond to it. The relevance of individual behavior to institutional process is illustrated in a simulation activity that offers students an opportunity to "walk through" a hypothetical conflict based on real historic circumstances and an actual institution, the UN Security Council.

Like Scrofani's (Selection 20), Raby's approach also emphasizes the concept of multiple alternatives, demonstrating that the most constructive approach to conflict is through the formulation and consideration of as wide a range of options as possible (see Selection 13). This notion of multiple possibilities and options is one that should also inform a futuristic approach to peace and conflict, as it does in the *Peacekeeping* exercise (Selection 21), and should as well be incorporated into futures imaging such as that described in the Bickmore curriculum (Selection 18). In fact, some may wish to plan a curriculum integrating elements of the three curricula into one course of study.

SELECTION 22
Conflict Resolution

Entrant: John Raby

School: The Governor's School of New Jersey on Public Issues and the Future of New Jersey, Monmouth College, Cedar Road, W. Long Branch, NJ 07764

Grade: Gifted high school seniors; adaptable for other high school students

Department or Subject: Interdisciplinary: course draws on ideas and information from history, political science, sociology, world order studies, psychology.

Concepts: There are a number of ways to perceive, define, analyze, and resolve conflict. The more we know about these possibilities, the greater the chance we can resolve conflict to the satisfaction of everyone concerned.

Topics: Definitions of conflict and peace; magnitude and types of conflict; personal involvement as it affects conflict resolution; how conflicts develop; motivating principles and objectives in resolving conflict; forms of reaction to conflict; operational frameworks for conflict resolution; summarizing conflict management/resolution strategies; the arms race; nonviolence in conflict resolution.

Materials: Various books, pamphlets, and articles both as texts and supplementary readings, the important starter for which is Ruth Leger Sivard's *World Military and Social Expenditures*; guest speakers, videotapes, handouts for in class exercise, tearoff sheets and magic markers, filmstrips.

Instructional Methods: Inductive questioning, creative problem-solving, simulation, story completion exercises, interviews with hosts on field trips and with guest speakers, field trips, showing audio-visuals, stu-

dent presentations, debriefing of all presentations and interviews, lecture and discussion. The point here is variety in order to engage everyone's interest.

Cognitive Objectives: At the end of the course, both in conversation and in
writing, students should be able to:

1. Offer clear definitions of conflict and peace
2. Systematically identify different levels of magnitude and types of
   conflict
3. Identify and describe different motives and goals in resolving conflict
4. Describe and compare different forms of reaction to conflict
5. Identify and analyze different ways of perceiving the arms race
6. Propose a means to resolve a conflict they choose to investigate

Affective Objectives:

1. Accept conflict as a fact of life.
2. Develop the patience to explore various ways of perceiving, reacting
   to, and resolving conflict.
3. Recognize conflict as a problem that might be solved as well as a
   threat.
4. Develop alternatives to win-lose approaches to conflict, as outlined
   in Fisher and Ury's *Getting To Yes* (which is now a basic text for the
   entire Governor's School student body, having started as the basic
   text in the conflict course in 1983).

OUTLINE

  I. Definitions of Conflict and Peace
 II. Scale of Conflict
     A. Within Individuals
     B. Between Individuals
     C. Between Groups
     D. Between Politically Sovereign Communities
III. Can Conflict and Peace Exist Simultaneously?
 IV. Types of Conflict
     A. Fights
     B. Games
     C. Debates
  V. Degree of Personal Involvement as a Consideration in Conflict Reso-
     lution
     A. First Party Conflict
     B. Second Party Conflict
     C. Third Party Conflict and Mediation

    VI. A Model for Tracing How Conflicts Develop
   VII. Motivating Principles and Objectives in Resolving Conflict
       A. Goodness
       B. Justice
          1. What is Fair?
          2. Can One Have Equality and Equity at the Same Time?
       C. Prudence
  VIII. Forms of Reaction to Conflict
       A. Threat or Problem-Oriented?
       B. Outwardly, Inwardly, or Passively Directed?
   IX. Operational Frameworks for Conflict Resolution
       A. Win-Lose
       B. Compromise
       C. Cooperation
    X. A Summary of Conflict Management/Resolution Strategies
   XI. Different Ways of Perceiving the Arms Race
  XII. Nonviolence: A Practical Approach to Resolving Conflict?

The above outline is more an indicator of the path we take than a list of errands to be completed. One facet of the course is its ability to adjust to the pace and inclination of the students. We spend as much time as the students need discussing any item on the outline, with no obligation to complete the list. Any student wishing to investigate a particular topic in depth could do so within the framework of tutorial sessions, devoted to extra help or discussion of individual projects. At the students' request, we reserve time during the last week of the course for reports on individual projects. Another option is a whole-class project, perhaps an investigation of various systems of national defense or a curriculum on the arms race. This project might be connected with the problem-solving portions of the evening series. [The program includes evenings as well as days — Ed.]

It is intended that everyone leave the course understanding that there are more and better things in conflict resolution than the choice between a grudging compromise and a fight.

Texts for the Course

    Ruth Leger Sivard, *World Military and Social Expenditures*, 1983 [This is an annual report; see Recommended Curriculum Materials listing].
    Gilbert S. Stubs, *How Realistic is the Nuclear Freeze Proposal?*
    David McReynolds, *Beyond the Freeze: Toward Abolition*

Roger Fisher, *International Conflict for Beginners* (New York: Harper & Row, 1970)

Donald B. Louria, M.D., "Consequences of Living in a Hair-Trigger Alert Era," *The Journal of the Medical Society of New Jersey*, August 1983

Supplemental Readings

International Seminar for Training in Nonviolent Action, *U.S. Defense Policy: Mainstream Views and Nonviolent Alternatives.*

James L. Adams, *Conceptual Blockbusting* (New York: Norton, 1980).

Robert Jay Lifton & Richard Falk, *Indefensible Weapons* (New York: Basic Books, 1982).

Anders Boserup & Andrew Mack, *War Without Weapons* (New York: Schocken, 1975).

Erik Erikson, *Childhood and Society* (New York: Norton, 1964).

Jonathan Schell, *The Fate of the Earth* (New York: Knopf, 1982).

Ernest W. Lefever & Stephen Hunt, eds., *The Apocalyptic Premise: Nuclear Arms Debated* (Washington, DC: Ethics and Public Policy, 1982).

Roger Fisher & William Ury, *Getting to Yes* (Boston: Houghton Mifflin, 1981).

Nuclear Education: Deterrence

In the conceptual framework for teaching about nuclear weapons presented in a special issue of *Social Education*, the authors note deterrence as one of the central and essential concepts of the framework (Jacobson, Reardon, & Sloan, 1983). However, the concept has not generally been featured in nuclear education curricula. Indeed, few of the major strategic concepts so fundamental to comprehending the "defense" postures of the nuclear powers are studied. Thus few students emerge from secondary schools with adequate understanding of international security issues.

M. Bruce King's "Nuclear War and the Arms Race" does feature a section on deterrence. The section is especially good because it encourages conceptual and analytic thinking. It asks students to define some of the major subconcepts and to reflect on how deterrence is intended to work. The materials employed are clearly and simply presented, well suited to the senior high school student or the average citizen. The entire curriculum contains handout readings and a number of well-designed exercises based on provocative ques-

tions, enabling the students to review the data and engage in significant reflection on its implications.

Teachers using this unit should review for inclusion materials that reflect a
position more favorable to the deterrence doctrine and that describe in more
detail the assumptions and values upon which deterrence theory is based. A
more global perspective might be developed by including some of the free,
simple materials published and distributed by the United Nations Department
for Disarmament Affairs (see Resource Organizations) and by reviewing some
of the nuclear disarmament proposals presented to the United Nations. For an
example of these materials, see Selection 24.

SELECTION 23
Nuclear War and the Arms Race

Entrant: M. Bruce King
School: Watertown Senior High School, 505 South 8th Street, Watertown,
WI 53094
Grade Level: Secondary (grades 10–12)
Subject: Social Studies/Alternative Learning Program
Concepts:
    Reducing the risk of nuclear war
    U.S.-Soviet cooperation
    Empowerment/effecting change
    Economic and social costs of the arms race
Topics: Immediate and long-term effects of nuclear war (including nuclear
    winter); history of the arms race and present military strength; national
    security; deterrence and negotiation; nuclear freeze campaign.
Materials: Bibliography:
    The Arms Race, David L. Bender, ed. St. Paul, MN: Greenhaven Press,
        1982.
    Beyond the Cold War, by E. P. Thompson. New York: Pantheon
        Books, 1982.
    Beyond the Freeze, by David Ford, Henry Kendall, and Steve Nades
        (Union of Concerned Scientists). Boston: Beacon Press, 1982.
    The Final Epidemic for all Living Things, brochure published by Physi-
        cians for Social Responsibility. Cambridge, MA.
    A Primer on the Nuclear Arms Race, booklet and poster by David Gold
        and Stephen Rose. Baltimore, MD: Social Graphics Co., 1983.
    "Militarism and Education," *Interracial Books for Children Bulletin*,
        13(6 & 7), 1982.
    "Taking Weapons to Court," *Nuclear Times*, February 1984.

Waging Peace, Jim Wallis, ed. San Francisco: Harper and Row, 1982.
"Wisconsin Magazine," videotape from WHA-TV, Madison, WI, April
    15, 1982.

Instructional Methods:
Unit prepared for individual study with small-group discussion. In-
    cludes directed reading activities, written activities, videotapes,
    and discussions.

Cognitive Objectives: Students will be able to:
    a. Define terms and concepts relating to nuclear war and the arms race
    b. Apply terms to new situations
    c. Analyze opposing viewpoints on the needs of national security
    d. Evaluate nuclear policy decisions and recommendations
    e. Describe the history of the arms race (1945–1985) and compare U.S.-
        USSR nuclear strength
    f. Evaluate actions and goals of anti-nuclear/peace groups
    g. Discuss immediate and long-term effects of nuclear war
    h. Examine economic and social costs of the arms race
    i. Analyze and evaluate alternatives for reducing the risk of nuclear war

Affective Objectives: The unit is designed to help students:
    a. Improve self-concept
    b. Understand the complexity and seriousness of the present world
        situation
    c. Feel a sense of hope for the future
    d. Develop an appreciation for and a willingness to accept their roles as
        political beings
    e. Value cooperation, interdependence, and nonviolence

MATERIAL DISTRIBUTED TO STUDENTS

Deterrence

1. Deterrence explained: "A deterrence or defensive strategy is based on
threatening massive and unacceptable retaliation against an aggressor if the
aggressor strikes first. It is based on the ability to strike back against cities
and factories that are sprawling targets and are vulnerable to any nuclear
blast. The weapons do not have to be accurate or sophisticated" [Robert
Aldrich, "The Deadly Race," in J. Wallis (ed.), *Waging Peace* (San Francisco: Harper & Row, 1982), p. 38].
    A. define: "strategy"
    B. define: "retaliation"
    C. define: "aggressor"

2. Based on the above paragraph, describe what deterrence is in your own words. See me if you need some help.

3. Now that you know what deterrence is, you should be able to apply it to a new situation. Let's say you have had a serious argument with another person your age. You fear that this person, in his anger, might try to inflict physical harm on you. If you followed a policy of deterrence, what would you do to try to prevent this person from attacking you? Why would you do this?

4. Would your actions solve the basic conflict between you and your "enemy"? Why or why not?

5. MAD explained: "This is, essentially, the political meaning of contemporary deterrence theory. In its pure form, that of MAD, or Mutual Assured Destruction, it proposes that war between the superpowers and their allies may be indefinitely postponed because nuclear weapons make any alternative unthinkable or unacceptable. I emphasize 'postponement.' The theory does not propose the resolution of those differences between the two parties which might, purportedly, bring them to war. On the contrary, by maintaining each party in a posture of menace to the other, it fixes indefinitely the tension which makes the resolution of differences improbable" [E. P. Thompson, *Beyond the Cold War* (New York: Harper & Row, 1982), pp. 1–2].

A. define: "mutual"

B. define: "assured"

C. define: "postpone"

D. define: "resolution"

6. According to this theory, what would happen if the Soviet Union attacked us with nuclear weapons?

7. Based on your knowledge of the nuclear capabilities of the U.S. and Soviet Union, do you think mutual assured destruction is the likely outcome of an attack by one country on the other?

8. "Because both countries fear mutual destruction if one country attacks the other, neither the U.S. nor the Soviet Union will ever use their nuclear weapons." Many people in both countries believe this statement to be true. Do you? Explain why or why not?

9. Based on your analysis so far, is the policy of deterrence by itself enough to prevent nuclear war?

10. The consequences of the policy of deterrence: "The elementary notion of deterrence—the cave men with their clubs, or a few ICBMs on each side—has a certain common-sense plausibility. It has even sometimes worked. But deterrence theory, in its scholastic or vulgar political expression, has long parted company with common-sense. By excluding all other phenomena, except the worst case, from view, it offers, always, weaponry as a substitute for the diplomatic or political resolution of differences. It freezes all political process and, increasingly, on both sides, constricts even cultural and intellectual exchanges within the same ideological parameters" (Thompson, p. 15).

    A. define: "plausibility"

    B. define: "diplomatic"

    C. define: "resolution"

    D. define: "constrict"

    11. What do you think is meant by: "weaponry [is] a substitute for the diplomatic and political resolution of differences"?

    12. "Negotiation" is a term we apply to the diplomatic and political resolution of differences. That is, discussion and compromise are used to try to solve problems between two countries in conflict. This is an alternative to the use of weapons to solve the problems. Look over the following actions and decide if each action is an example of deterrence (D) or negotiation (N).

____ a. USSR places nuclear missiles in Cuba (1962).

____ b. President Reagan meets with Soviet minister of Defense (1984).

____ c. Secretary of Defense Weinberger asks Congress to increase military budget (1984).

____ d. President Reagan supports research on anti-missile satellites (1983).

____ e. Presidential candidate Mondale proposes a yearly meeting with the Soviets (1984).

____ f. President Nixon meets with Soviet leader Brezhnev to discuss reductions in nuclear arms (1969).

____ g. The U.S. and USSR agree to the Nuclear Test Ban Treaty (1963).

____ h. The U.S. places Cruise and Pershing missiles in Western Europe and the USSR responds by placing more missiles in Eastern Europe (1982).

____ i. The USSR launches the first rocket into space (Sputnik) and the U.S. responds by increasing development of new technology (1957).

____ j. Many U.S. and Soviet citizens support a bilateral freeze on the building of new nuclear weapons (1984).

Probing Nuclear Weapons Issues

Fact Sheet 17, from the series of information pamphlets published and distributed free of charge by the United Nations Department for Disarmament Affairs (see Resource Organizations), is a very brief comprehensive summary of a UN experts' report that the editor believes would be very useful in second-ary courses such as "Nuclear War and the Arms Race." The following questions are based upon the Fact Sheet. We suggest teachers write for free copies and conduct a class discussion using these questions, which originally appeared in *Ways and Means*, Fall 1978, published by the Institute for World Order (no longer available).

SELECTION 24
Study on Nuclear Weapons

Source: Fact Sheet 17, U.N. Department for Disarmament Affairs

1. What do the facts cited in the opening excerpt [see Selection 23] suggest about preparation for civil defense in case of nuclear attack?

2. Were you previously aware of the effects of nuclear weapons? If so, how did you become aware? Do most people you know have this information? Do you believe the public in general should be informed about the effects of nuclear weapons? Does knowledge of these effects influence your opinion on the role of nuclear weapons in national security policy? Does it affect your opinions on disarmament? Explain these influences. Does it seem to you that these effects would, in fact, cripple or destroy human society? Why or why not?

3. How could "first strike capability" cause deterrence to fail? How could such capability change the balance that is believed to prevent nuclear war? How might a severe crisis affect these strategic doctrines?

4. Why was the 1946 UN resolution on the complete prohibition of nuclear weapons never implemented? In your opinion, have the agreements on specific arms control objectives contributed to or detracted from the achievement of general and complete disarmament? Explain your opinion and indicate how you believe your conclusions could or should influence the deliberations of SSDII. (This last sentence refers to the UN's Second Special Session on Disarmament held in 1982.)

5. Why is it that so many scientists involved in the scientific discoveries that led to the development of nuclear weapons, such as Niels Bohr, have called for international control over nuclear technology? What role could or should scientists play in the control of nuclear weapons? Do you agree that "mankind is hostage to the perceived security of a few nuclear weapons states?" Why do they maintain that perception? Do you believe that these states are more or less or just as secure as non–nuclear weapons states? Why? If you do agree with the hostage statement, what suggestions can you make to liberate the hostage? Can information and education contribute to the liberation process? If so, how?

Global Issues: Problem Solving

The tenth-grade course in Global Education by Maryanne Schiller and Ernani Falcone of Upper Merion High School offers a particularly useful model of the problem-solving approach. It also provides some helpful specific procedures for problem identification, analytic discussion, and attitude assessment.

The rationale that introduces the curriculum—under the heading, "Analysis of the End Sought"—emphasizes the development of an ongoing inquiry approach to problem solving. It is included here because peace educators should find it and the problem solution criteria it lists useful and adaptable to the study of a wide range of global problems. The list of "Learning Objectives" provides further insights into problem-solving operations and processes, as does the student handout, which is a good model description of what students can expect from the unit and what will be expected of them. It demonstrates a participatory approach and clearly assigns a large portion of the responsibility for learning to the students themselves. The interactive element is a form of cooperative learning that enables students to undertake their learning tasks in a community-building fashion.

Teachers might consider adding to this curriculum an experiential dimension in which the students could apply its techniques and solutions to relevant problems in the school, the community, or the national or global spheres. They might also develop their own sets of criteria for what constitutes a good problem solution.

SELECTION 25
Global Education

Entrant: Maryanne Schiller and Ernani Falcone
School: Upper Merion High School, Crossfield Rd., King of Prussia, PA
    19406
Grade Level: 10
Subject: Social Studies
Concepts: Global Citizenship, Problem Solving
Topics Covered: Rapid population growth; arms race; resource scarcity; environmental decay
Materials: Text: John Molyneux and Marilyn Olsen, *World Prospects* (Scar-

borough, Ont.: Prentice-Hall of Canada, 1979). Each topic is based upon a particular set of resources used. Information can be made available upon request.

Instructional Methods: Lecture, simulations, developing cognitive maps, debates, paper writing for evaluation — no formal memorization tests.

Cognitive Objectives:

Problem solving skills: inferring effects; anticipating effects; inferring causes; setting criteria; analyzing alternative solutions; evaluating solutions; taking a stand; developing, doing, and evaluating personal plans.

General Concepts: interdependence, alternative futures, global awareness.

Information: related to four areas under study; topic changes every 9 weeks (each quarter).

Affective Objectives:

Pretest of attitudes

Cognitive learning on problem solving

Actually developing, doing, and evaluating a personal plan of action

Posttest of attitudes

Attitudes analyzed:

1. Willingness to take social action.
2. Willingness to promote taking social action by others.

ANALYSIS OF THE END SOUGHT

"As a direct result of participating in the World Cultures/Global Education Course . . . "

Since people learn by doing, the World Cultures/Global Education Course is designed to provide students with opportunities to practice the behaviors described in the End Sought Statement and to integrate these behaviors into a total life-related task.

". . . students demonstrate a willingness and an ability . . ."

The intent of the World Cultures/Global Education Course is that students develop not only the knowledge and skills necessary to perform certain life tasks efficiently, but also the commitment to use them for some beneficial purpose. The assumption underlying this part of the End Sought Statement is that attitudes form as a result of behavior. Since learning is, by definition, a change in behavior, it follows that the World Cultures/Global Education Course, by producing observable positive changes in student behavior, will also produce observable positive changes in student attitude. The ends sought by the World Cultures/Global Education Course are described in terms of behavior in the Criterion Task, the successful performance of which will require students to demonstrate the desired behaviors at an acceptable level of achievement.

". . . to analyze global situations and identify world problems, . . ."

A *world problem* is defined . . . as a situation which threatens the quality and/or existence of life on earth . . . caused by global factors. . . . This course provides students opportunities to analyze selected world situations, that is, to examine them in terms of their causes and effects.

". . . determine and justify their personal positions on different proposed solutions . . ."

. . . This kind of decision making requires the student to analyze the situation and define the world problem, identify the standards which must be met by any proposed solutions in terms of their anticipated results, and evaluate the proposed solutions on the basis of how likely it appears that they will achieve the desired results, meet the identified standards, and operate under the existing conditions. . . .

". . . and contribute to effective solutions to world problems."

. . . Human survival depends upon the willingness of every member of society to contribute to an effective solution to world problems. An effective solution is one which closely conforms to the description of the *ideal solution*.[1]

IDEAL SOLUTIONS

An *ideal solution* is one which meets the following criteria:

1) Leads to the achievement of the *preferred state*
2) Eliminates the causes of the selected world problem
3) Does not have a negative effect on other world problems
4) Does not create other problems
5) Takes into consideration the conditions that must exist for the solution to work[2]

Each criterion of an *ideal solution* is explained in detail below.

Criterion one.   An *ideal solution* contributes to the achievement of the *preferred state*.

---

[1]It is suggested that the concept of an "ideal solution" should be replaced with that of "effective" or "preferred" as these terms tend to connote more possibility of achievement — Ed.

[2]Teachers may wish to compare the conceptual similarities between these criteria and the questions raised for evaluation of peacekeeping systems (Selection 21) — Ed.

In order to clarify the aim of the problem-solving situation, a problem solver must develop a specific vision of what the world would be like if the problem were solved.[3] Otherwise, a solution may be selected that appears effective in some ways but actually will not lead to the desired outcome. The World Cultures/Global Education Course defines this desired outcome as the *preferred state*. The *preferred state*, in relation to *rapid population growth*, for example, is a situation in which everyone has enough resources to meet basic needs and to pursue further human development.

Criterion two.   An *ideal solution* eliminates the causes of the selected world problem.

Too often, solutions address the symptoms of a problem without attending to its root causes. Such solutions have no lasting value. For example, attempts to solve the problem of domestic oil shortages by importing more foreign oil have not succeeded in solving the problem because at least one cause of the shortage, increasing levels of demand for a limited resource, has not been addressed. A more effective solution would aim at eliminating the cause of the oil shortage by finding an alternative source of energy, thus eliminating this cause of the problem of oil shortages by reducing the high demands for this limited resource.[4]

Criterion three.   An *ideal solution* does not have a negative effect on other world problems.

The solution to any one of the significant problems facing the world today depends to some extent on the solution of others.[5] For example, the problem of world poverty cannot be solved unless something is done about the world energy crisis. Often an attempt to alleviate one problem may make another problem more severe. For example, foreign aid to less developed countries has aimed at economic development based on conventional forms of energy. The result is an increased demand for and further shortages of this limited commodity in developing nations. Thus, this solution to the problem of poverty has exacerbated the problem of oil shortages. What is needed is a strategy directed toward solving a world problem without at the same time adversely affecting other world problems.

----

[3]This assertion is a significant rationale for the use of imaging (Selection 18) and model-building techniques (Selection 21) — Ed.

[4]This assertion is fundamental to the futuristic approach of imaging and model building, particularly characteristic of world order studies — Ed.

[5]This assertion reflects the concepts of global interdependence and the interrelatedness of problems, which are common to both global and peace education — Ed.

Criterion four.   An *ideal solution* does not create other problems.

Often solutions create new situations that are less desirable than the original problem situation. For example, an attempt to solve the energy crisis by the development of nuclear energy is creating wastes that pose an unprecedented threat to the natural environment. A growing number of people throughout the world feel this other threat to their well-being violates their human right to a healthful environment now and is a danger that must not be passed on to future generations. They feel this cure is worse than the disease. A more effective approach to energy shortages would provide fuel through an environmentally sound technology such as solar panels.

Criterion five.   An *ideal solution* takes into consideration the conditions that must exist for the solution to work.

When planners anticipate the success of their solution to a problem, they frequently fail to consider fully those factors, or conditions, that have a direct bearing on the results of the plan. Conditions can be classified in many ways: cultural, political, social, technological, logistical, environmental, economic, etc. One proposed solution to the oil shortage is to encourage Americans to voluntarily conserve gasoline. For this plan to be effective, certain conditions must exist. For example, there must be a change in the American cultural attitude toward the autonomy, convenience, and status afforded by owning and operating a private automobile. A logistical condition that must exist is an improvement in the mass transit systems that will provide Americans with an adequate alternate means of transportation. These are but two of many conditions that must be considered in planning an effective solution.

TAKING ACTION

In order to contribute to an effective solution to a world problem, a person must take action based on a carefully designed and justified personal plan. The individual must be able to evaluate both the planning and the actions on an ongoing basis. In order to provide students with repeated opportunities to practice this kind of behavior, the World Cultures/Global Education Course comprises a recycling of the following steps in problem solving:

1. Analyze the situation and define the problem.
2. Identify the five criteria that must be met by any proposed solution if it is to be effective.
3. Propose different personal plans of action and analyze them in terms of their anticipated results.

4. Choose the proposed plan of action that appears most likely to meet the identified criteria.
5. Implement the selected personal plan of action, evaluate the plan and the results of the personal action in terms of effectiveness, and recommend improvement of future planning and courses of action.

A totally effective solution to the problems of the world requires cooperation on a global level, but the effort must begin with the individual. The intent of the World Culture/Global Education Course is to provide students with the opportunity to practice the requried behaviors so that they will develop both the ability and the commitment to become politically active in a way that will promote the global unity necessary to bring people and nature into a harmonious balance.

LEARNING OBJECTIVES

Listed below are the thinking processes that can be observed in student behaviors, along with samples of questions that help elicit these behaviors.

Observing: What are some things you notice in the upper left hand corner of the Course Overview? [Not reproduced here.]

Recalling: What is meant by the term "rationale"?

Consulting: What do authorities say is likely to happen in the future if the problem of Rapid Population Growth continues to exist?

Classifying: What makes the problem of Rapid Population Growth a *world problem*?

Inferring Attributes: What would the world be like if the problem of Rapid Population Growth could be solved to everyone's satisfaction?

Anticipating: What else do you think will happen if supra-national agencies are created to solve world problems?

Making Choices: Which of the two proposed solutions to Rapid Population Growth is the more effective?

Noticing Similarities: What do all four situations have in common?

Noticing Differences: What are the differences between the four decisions?

SAMPLE LEARNING ACTIVITY PLAN
"BECOMING INFORMED AND TAKING A POSITION"

Purpose/rationale. To provide students an overview of the World Cultures/Global Education Course. (Before beginning the course, students need to have enough information about what they will be doing to satisfy their immediate curiosity and enough information about why what they will be doing is important to give them a reason for participating.)

Observable student behavior.   Students obtain and record information about the World Cultures/Global Education Course.

Content.   Information about what students will be doing in the course; information about why what they will be doing is important.

Student materials.   Student handout entitled *World Culture/Global Education: Course Overview*.

Learning strategy.   Data-gathering/retrieval

Teaching strategy.   Provide an overview of the entire course. For example, the teacher might say:
"In just a few years, each of you will be taking your place as a full-fledged adult member of society. This means you'll have a lot more privileges, but also a lot more responsibilities. And the responsibilities are very serious indeed. The decisions you make and the actions you take, both individually and as a contributing member of society, will be literally matters of life or death, not only for you and your family and friends, but for everyone on earth now and in the future.
"There have always been serious problems in the world — wars, famines, pestilences, natural disasters — but until this century, they have been temporary and confined to limited areas. Never before have the problems been so many, so big, and so interrelated that they have threatened the very existence of life on this planet. You know the names of some of these problems — the energy shortage, the nuclear threat, the arms race, hunger, pollution. You know something about most of them. You've even suffered some inconveniences and discomforts from most of them. And it's certain that you are going to become even more intimately acquainted with them in the future, whether you like it or not.
"But knowing something about these problems is not enough. Someone — and that someone is you and other members of the global society working together — has to come up with some effective solutions to these problems so that you and future generations will be assured not only of survival, but improved quality of life.
"What do you have to be able to do in order to come up with workable solutions to problems like the ones now facing the world? First of all, you must be able to research the problems to find out their causes and effects,

what's being done about them, and how these ways of attacking the problem are working — or not working. And if they're not working — or not working well enough — you must be able to figure out *why* they're not working as they should. You must also be able to propose some alternative ways of attacking the problem that will work better.

"You must be able to anticipate the consequences of taking one action or another and be able to choose the wise course. And finally, you must be able to take action — actually contribute to the effort to solve these problems, constantly re-evaluating and re-adjusting your actions to fit the changing situation.

"How do you learn to *do* these things? You learn to do them by doing them — just like you learned to walk and talk and ride a bicycle and drive a car. The purpose of this course is to give you some experience in actually *doing* these things — practicing the tasks that you will be called on to perform throughout life. And by *doing* them, you will be learning *how* to do them.

"And now I'm going to give each of you a sheet containing information that will answer some of the questions you may have about this course and perhaps remind you of some other questions you'd like to ask."

Distribute the student handout of the Course Overview. Discuss the handout with the students; for example:

"Someone, read aloud for us what it says in the space labeled 'Purpose.' . . . What words in the statement of purpose are unclear to you? . . . What questions do you have about what the statement of purpose means? . . . Someone, tell us in your own words what you think that means so I can be sure it is clear to everyone . . . [if necessary, give further clarification]. What questions do some of you still have about the purpose of the course? . . ."

Continue to discuss the Course Overview, one section at a time, using questions similar to the examples given above. Clarify and elaborate as needed.

Values and Learning Objectives

The seriousness with which peace education programs respond to opportunities for reasoned values analysis is perhaps best reflected in the learning objectives they espouse. Obviously the normative and attitudinal nature of the field will be reflected in the affective objectives the programs set forth. However, it is in the cognitive objectives that responsibility to the social values fundamental to citizenship education is best reflected. If peace education is to be the vehicle for social education for global citizenship, it, too, must espouse the objectives of Thomas Determan's tenth-grade curriculum. The full set of objectives provides an outstandingly comprehensive list of the learning goals for peace education (which all peace educators might study to assess their own programs and objectives). Special attention is called to the skills of listening and observing.

The curriculum is also exemplary in its matching of objectives, particularly skills, with topics of study and teaching methods. The issues and themes outlined offer a fine secondary level introduction to peace education.

SELECTION 26
Global Issues

Entrant: Thomas J. Determan
School: Hempstead High School, 3715 Pennsylvania Avenue, Dubuque, IA
52001
Grade Level: 10th grade
Subject: Social studies
Concepts: Global interdependence and global citizenship
Topics:

1. Interdependence	6. Economic Development
2. Cultural Linkages	7. Global Population Patterns
3. Foreign Policy	8. Conflict Resolution
4. Nuclear Arms Dilemma	9. Human Rights
5. International Organization	10. Global Environment

Materials: See relevant pages of the curriculum under "Activities and Resources."
Instructional Methods:

1. Background lectures	6. Guest speakers
2. Simulations	7. Students represent nations as diplomats
3. Audio-visual materials	
4. Panel/debates	8. Community research
5. Data analysis	9. Role-playing
	10. Newspaper discussion/ analysis

Type of Learner: Motivated; above-average reader; activity-oriented
Course Objectives: The student will:
1. Be able to develop a global perspective concerning issues, trends, ideas, and the nations of the world.
2. Be able to define the meaning of the Interdependence of Nations.

3. Define culture and identify the cultural differences among peoples of the world.
4. Develop an understanding of how his/her daily activities and quality of life are affected by global interaction of peoples and nations.
5. Be able to list the types of interactions between peoples and nations in the areas of technology, military security, ecology, culture, economic exchange, and personal freedoms.
6. Be able to identify the links between Dubuque, Iowa (or other home town), the United States, and the world in the areas of culture, economics, technology, environment, population, and resources.[1]
7. Demonstrate an understanding of the meaning of foreign policy and what impact it has on a nation's global relationships.
8. Be able to explain the history, issues, and alternatives of the nuclear arms dilemma.
9. Be able to discuss the importance of international organizations in keeping world peace.
10. Be able to explain the historical growth, current statistics, and distribution and social impact of the world population situation.
11. Be able to compare and contrast the situations in various nations concerning the issues of human rights, and be able to evaluate these situations in light of established international human rights provisions.
12. Be able to explain the nature of human conflict on the personal, group, and global levels.
13. Be able to discuss the causes and complexities of, and possible alternatives to, selected regional conflicts in the world.
14. Be able to extrapolate ideas on a global future through the analysis of global data and trends.

LEARNING OBJECTIVES

Attitudes

I. Understanding of self and others
   A. Accepting social differences
   B. Setting realistic goals
   C. Awareness that every individual has worth

---

[1]Such local-to-global links are the basis of the prototype study, "Columbus and the World," by Chadwick Alger of the Ohio State University. Curriculum materials to pursue this objective are available from Global Perspectives, Inc. (see Resource Organizations) — Ed.

D. Treating every individual with tolerance and respect

E. Treating others with justice and fairness

F. Respecting other countries, people, and ways of life

G. Appreciating the contributions of many different people to life in the U.S.

H. Showing openmindedness toward new or unfamiliar ideas, points of view, etc.

II. Responsibility

A. Developing a sense of individual responsibility

B. Accepting responsibility

III. Relationships

A. Asking questions about human affairs and seeking answers to them.

B. Lawfully protesting unjust rules, laws, or authority, calling attention to them and opposing them through use of the democratic system.

IV. Students will learn to think through values issues by considering alternative modes of thinking and acting.

A. Weighing pros and cons of alternatives

B. Recognizing consequences of alternatives

V. Students will be better prepared to make appropriate choices, based on knowledge and consideration of values.

VI. Students will be provided with a process for selecting the best and rejecting the worst elements of the various value systems which confront them.

VII. Students will be more able to bring their beliefs and actions into harmony.

VIII. Students will apply the valuing/decision-making process to their own lives.

IX. Students will have an increased understanding of the importance of openness, acceptance, and respect among groups and individuals.

Skills

I. Reference and Location Skills

A. Use index

B. Use glossary, appendix, map lists, and illustration lists

C. Choose appropriate meaning of words for the context in which used

D. Recognize various materials as sources of information about different topics

E. Locate appropriate material in a library

    F. Use headings, topic sentences, and summary sentences

    G. Locate information through cross-references

    H. Use reference material such as atlases, *World Almanac*, and *Reader's Guide*

    I. Select important current events items

    J. Select information pertinent to class activities from various materials

    K. Use card catalogue to find materials listed by subject, author, and title

    L. Utilize various sections of material

    M. Skim while reading to find a particular word, get a general impression, or locate specific information

II. Listening and Observing (interviews, field trips, lectures, play, panel discussions, etc., in or outside the classroom)

    A. Listen and observe with a purpose

    B. Listen attentively while others are speaking

    C. Plan rules of behavior, questions to be asked, and things to look for

    D. Reserve judgment until the speaker's entire presentation is completed

    E. Listen carefully to a presentation and be able to recall and reproduce the basic main idea and important details

III. Organizing Information

    A. Classify facts and events under main headings or in categories

    B. Compose a title for a story, picture graph, map, or chart

    C. Select answers to questions from material heard, viewed, or read

    D. Record and summarize information gained

    E. Select main ideas and supporting facts

    F. Arrange events, facts, and ideas in chronological sequence

    G. Take notes to make a record of a source by author, title, and page

    H. Give credit for quoted material

    I. Be able to take clear, accurate, useful notes

IV. Study Skills

    A. Ability to use individual capacities as fully as possible

    B. Knowledge of the basic secondary school social studies information sources

    C. Ability to use these information sources

V. Evaluating Information

    A. Distinguish between fact and fiction

    B. Draw inferences and make generalizations from evidence

    C. Compare information from two or more sources to recognize agreement or contradiction

VI. Communicating Ideas
  A. Exchange ideas through discussion as leader or participant
  B. Respect limitations of time and the right of others to be heard
  C. Use notes in preparing and presenting ideas
VII. Working with Others
  A. Respect the rights and opinions of others
  B. Understand the need for rules and the necessity of observing them
VIII. Applying Problem Solving and Critical Thinking
  A. Define a problem for study
  B. Review known information about the problem
  C. Locate, gather, and organize information
  D. Interpret and evaluate information
  E. Summarize and draw tentative conclusions; make tentative decision
  F. Recognize the need to change conclusions when new information warrants
  G. Predict consequences of each tentative decision
  H. Recognize areas for further study
IX. Interpreting Maps and Globes
  A. Use different map projections
  B. Know the major advantages of the various map projections.
  C. Use globe effectively in social studies work
X. Map Location
  A. Recognize land and water masses
  B. Use an atlas
  C. Develop a visual image of major political divisions, land forms, and other map patterns
  D. Read maps of various types
  E. Be able to use graphs, charts, and time lines
XI. Understanding Chronology
  A. Relate the past to the present in the study of change and continuity in human affairs
  B. Associate some specific dates/events as points of orientation in time
  C. Use definite time concepts, such as decade and century
  D. Learn to fomulate generalizations and conclusions about time in studying the development of human affairs

COURSE OUTLINE

I. An Introduction to the Global Village
  A. What is a global perspective?
  B. History of the state

C. Interaction between people: Learning about human conflict
II. Interdependence
  A. World systems
  B. Links to the world
    1. U.S.
    2. Iowa [i.e., home state]
    3. Dubuque [i.e., home town]
  C. J-curves
  D. Application of interdependence to contemporary events
III. Cultural links
  A. Changing views of ourselves in the universe
  B. People as insiders and outsiders
  C. Differing human viewpoints
  D. Communication
  E. Cultural patterns: old and new ways
IV. Foreign policy
  A. Definition
  B. Variables influencing foreign policy
  C. Foreign policy models
    1. United States
    2. Tanzania
    3. USSR
  D. Foreign policy dilemma: a simulation
  E. Foreign policy speeches
  F. History of U.S. foreign policy
V. Nuclear arms
  A. History of warfare prior to 1945
  B. Nuclear chronology
  C. Nuclear arms issues
  D. Effects of nuclear war
  E. A futuristic nuclear war scenario
VI. International organization[2]
  A. Concert of Europe
  B. Systems of international organization
    1. Collective security—League of Nations
    2. Collective force—UN
    3. Limited world government
  C. Evaluation of systems
VII. Global economic development

[2]This section is based in part on the materials used for the peacekeeping models (Selection 21)—Ed.

A. Life in third world
B. Comparison of 1st, 2nd and 3rd worlds—statistics
C. Activities of economic development
D. Development: case studies
E. Role of foreign assistance
F. UN development conference: a simulation
VIII. Global population patterns
A. History of human population growth
B. Current global population situation
C. Population pyramids
D. Food supply: relationship to population growth
E. Differing perspectives on global population situation
IX. Human rights[3]
A. Defining human rights
B. Historical perspectives on human rights in the East and the West
C. Cross-cultural comparisons of human rights documents
D. UN Universal Declaration of Human Rights
E. Global issues of human rights
F. Apartheid: a case study
X. Keeping the peace
A. Human conflict
B. Conflict case studies
1. Arab-Israeli conflict
2. Conflict in Central America
C. U.S. role

Global Issues: Diagnosing the International System

Peace education seeks to develop a critical awareness of world problems and a global perspective on their resolution. Critical awareness and a global perspective characterize the approach of the senior elective history course by Peter Schmidt and Michael Chimes of Gill St. Bernard's School.

"International Relations" gives an excellent grounding in the international state system, which is essential to understanding contemporary world politics, and calls upon students to actively participate in the analysis and projection of policy-making. In this process, students are led through a reasoned analysis of

[3]Teachers seeking further curricular suggestions on human rights may contact The Human Rights Center, School of International Affairs, Columbia University, New York, NY 10027—Ed.

policy alternatives. Based upon an excellent set of readings, this curriculum deals with one major issue of growing importance no other curriculum treated, terrorism.

Critical capacity is developed through the examination of bias, the exploration of conflicting and contradictory information, and the study of policy alternatives. The capacity is exercised and tested as students formulate their own policy proposals.

Only the first half of the full semester course is excerpted here.

It is recommended that educators who are considering the development of a course along these lines set it within the global context and raise explicit critical questions about the international system from the outset. This might be done by adding the World Policy Institute (see Resource Organizations) Working Paper #20, "The Struggle for a Just World Order: An Agenda of Inquiry and Praxis for the 1980's," to the introductory readings. Also recommended is the addition of a unit on futures projections of preferred systems based on the Bickmore (Selection 18) and/or *Peacekeeping* (Selection 21) exercises.

SELECTION 27
International Relations

Entrant: Peter Schmidt and Michael Chimes
School: Gill St. Bernard's School, P.O. Box 239, Bernardsville, NJ 07924
Grade Level: Senior elective
Department or Subject: History
Concepts: The students are encouraged to think and act as policymakers in the area of international relations. The approach to the course is both academic and action-oriented. It is not merely a study of international issues.
Topics: The course is divided into 8 areas: Introduction; The International Setting; Issues of International Development; Superpower Relations and the Arms Race; Areas of International Concern: 1. The Middle East, 2. Central America, 3. South Africa; Conclusions — A Look at the Future
Materials: The Great Powers (Cannon et al.), *A Map History of Our Times* (Catchpole), *The Developing World* (World Bank), *Real Security* (Barnet), *The Arms Race* (Bender), *The Nuclear Delusion* (Kennan), *A Compassionate Peace* (Amer. Friends Service Comm.), *The Middle East* (Leone), *The Nicaragua Reader* (Fried, Gettleman), *El Salvador* (Gettleman), *A Window on Soweto* (Sikakane), *Focus on South Africa* (Intercom #105)

Instructional Methods: The course uses lectures, seminar discussions, films
and videotapes, simulation games, field trips to organizations involved
in international relations, and interviews with people engaged in this
work.

Cognitive Objectives: In terms of information, students will become familiar with the interrelationship of nations both globally and regionally.
Specific study will focus on the common issues and concerns that tie
these nations together. In terms of skills, particular attention will be
paid to the skill of reviewing contradictory primary and secondary
source material and evaluating it.

Affective Objectives: Students will become aware of their biases in terms of
their perceptions of international relations. Students will become aware
of their potential as citizens in a democratic system, and learn ways they
can translate this potential into social and political action. Students will
see international relations not in terms of American foreign affairs, but
rather from the perspectives of various nations.

STUDENT'S SYLLABUS

Course Objectives

A study of recent developments in international affairs, this course will
explore the theories, principles, and practices that govern modern relations
among nations. The course will attempt to provide an understanding of how
the present system of international relations functions, as well as an appreciation of major problems that the world faces at the present time. Finally, we
will explore some of the possible roles that various nations may play in
efforts to solve these critical issues. . . .

In terms of content, we will examine aspects of international diplomacy
as they presently exist: the function of world organizations such as the
United Nations; issues of war and peace; current problems in the Middle
East, Central America, and South Africa; the impact of U.S.-Soviet relations on world affairs; and, in conclusion, anticipate how international
relations may develop and play a role in maintaining or creating a new world
order as we approach the 21st century. By the conclusion of the course
students should be able to understand that the problems that we face today
are global in nature and can be solved only through considerable international attention.

The course is also designed to assist students in becoming involved as
responsible citizens in solving these complex issues. Written assignments are

to be presented as peace proposals for each of the major areas that we will be studying. You will note that many of the assignments require the student to contact people in organizations that are working to resolve problems and conflicts. We expect your full participation in these efforts.

Course Overview

Part one.   Introduction to the Course (Jan. 3, 4). Readings (all class handouts):

"An Introduction to International Relations," by Frederick Hartmann
"The Eight Schools of American Foreign Policy"
"Dictatorships and Double-Standards," by Jeane Kirkpatrick (*Commentary*, November 1979)

Part two.   The International Setting and the Evolution of the State System (Jan. 7–11, 15–18). Topics to be discussed:

1. Theories of the origin of the state
2. Introduction to international relations from World War I until World War II
3. Introduction to international relations since WWII
4. An introduction to the concept of superpowers
5. Simulation game — "Firebreaks"
6. The role of international organizations
7. The role of alliances
8. The role of the non-aligned nations

Readings: *The Great Powers*, by Cannon, Clark, and Smuga; *A Map History of Our Times*, by Catchpole
Proposal (to be done together): A conference on the issue of international terrorism. We will be doing several class readings together on the topic of international terrorism. Together we will attempt to define terrorism — few people agree on precisely what it is — and discuss the relationships between it and the social, economic, and political conditions from which it arises. Using the readings and political writings that have been handed out as background information, construct a proposal on "International Terrorism: What Can be Done?" Who are terrorists and what is the basis of their actions? Is there a difference between terrorism and political violence? Is terrorism ever justified? Under what circumstances? Is terrorism an international issue or is it only a matter of concern for a few nations? What do you

propose as a possible solution to the problem? How would you implement your proposal?

Part three.   Issues of International Development (Jan. 21–25, Jan. 28–Feb. 1, Feb. 4–8). Topics to include:

1. Issues of international development
2. Case studies of Third World development — Kenya, Mexico, and India
3. The transnational economy
4. Issues of underdevelopment — whose responsibility?

Films to include: "And Who Shall Feed the World?" (NBC documentary on the role of the United States in solving world hunger); "Controlling Interest: The Multinational Corporations" (an analysis of the multinational corporations and their roles in developing nations).

Readings: *The Developing World* and *The Development Data Book*, both by the World Bank, and *Real Security*, by Richard J. Barnet

Proposal: Choose a nation or region of the world that our reading has identified as underdeveloped. Writing your essay in two parts, first describe the nation or region in terms of its specific problems — rely on the information from *The Development Data Book* — and how and why those problems have arisen and developed. In the second part of your essay, propose a specific plan of action that addresses these problems. Keep in mind the role of the national government (or regional governments), the potential use of outside assistance from other nations, and the role of international agencies and organizations such as the World Bank, the United Nations, etc.

Part four.   Superpower relations and the nuclear arms race (Feb. 11–15, Feb. 25–Mar. 1). Topics to include:

1. U.S.-Soviet relations in historical perspective
2. Concepts of balance of power
3. The challenges confronting the United States
4. The challenges confronting the Soviet Union
5. The arms race: myths and realities
6. Arms control and disarmament: a historical perspective

Films to include: "Gods of Metal" (an analysis of the arms race from a Christian perspective, emphasizing the effects on the poor around the world); "George Kennan: A Critical Choice" (possible alternatives to the arms race).

Readings: *The Arms Race*, Opposing Viewpoints Series; *The Nuclear Delusion*, by George Kennan

Proposal: Write a proposal as an American student on the role of education in enabling the United States and the Soviet Union to realize closer relations with one another. In your proposal, take the time to critique your own education—what have its strengths and weaknesses been in terms of your being able to understand the Soviet Union and the issue of the arms race? What assistance have specific subjects been? Anything detrimental? Following this analysis, interview three high school students from other schools to determine their thinking on the subject. In your conclusions, use the following quotation from George Kennan to guide your thinking on the subject:

> Let us therefore, instead of becoming discouraged by the darkness of the moment and by our helplessness over the recent past, redouble our efforts on behalf of world peace, remembering that what is required of us first of all is the acquisition and dissemination of a greater understanding of ourselves and of the inherent tendencies of our own society, a greater understanding of those whom so many of us have learned to regard as our enemies, but without whose willing collaboration, no world peace will be conceivable at all.

Global Issues: War as an Institution

The problems of war as an institution and/or a system is addressed by John W. Ryder in "Global Studies—An Inquiry Course," taught at Boonton High School by Walter J. Angilly.

The course is well structured, yet adaptable to the inclusion of other materials. It is especially sound conceptually, basing its approach on knowledge derived from peace research with its use of the conceptualization of "positive" and "negative peace."

Teachers may wish to vary the presentation-lecture format moving from a teacher led process to more student generated inquiry, including some group work. Some may also wish to include some of the recent work on economic conversion from military to civilian spending and production. Consideration of past, present, and futuristic proposals for alternative security systems (Galtung, 1984; Sommer, 1985) might also be added.

In order to implement the unit as excerpted here, teachers will need to order the transparencies, which offer graphs and diagrams of the basic concepts and data used in the course, from Mr. Angilly at Boonton High School.

As presented, however, the unit offers an excellent outline for a study of the war system.

SELECTION 28
Global Studies: An Inquiry Course

Entrant: John W. Ryder
School: Boonton High School, 306 Lathrop Avenue, Boonton, NJ 07005
Grade Level: Senior high school and Continuing Education
Department: Social studies
Concepts:
   World Systems and interrelated global problems
   Social problem analysis
   World citizen judgment skills
   Human survival and enhancement in an interdependent age
Topics:
   Basic Data on the Human Habitat; Self/Species/Planet Relationships;
   Definitions; How We Think; Today, A Totally New Era in History;
   Spaceship Earth; War/Peace Problems; Ecological Damage; Economic
   Resources and Development; Human Rights; Population, Food, Ener-
   gy; Centers of Power; International Organization; Future
Materials: Color transparencies or slides for all units. [These are provided
   with the entire course of study, available as noted in the introduction
   that precedes this entry.]
Instructional Methods: The approach is that of the inquiry method of teach-
   ing and learning based upon timely and meaningful questions and
   dialogue.
Cognitive Objectives:
   To increase knowledge of world systems
   To reinforce analytical skills and behaviors
   To improve judgment making
   To enhance visual frames of reference
   To integrate knowledge for human survival
Affective Objectives:
   Pursue an integrated study of the current world scene
   View the interwoven future of self/species/planet relationships
   Develop an increased respect and concern for Human Species as a
       whole
   Begin, in matters which are relevant, to be an effective and responsible

contributor(s) to the decision-making processes of the political and other institutions of the community, state, country, and world

THE WAR-PEACE PROBLEM
A 15-Day Unit

Objectives

A. To learn the meaning of basic terms
B. To know the causes of 20th century wars
C. To review humankind's efforts toward peace
D. To realize the nature of nuclear war
E. To examine the arms race and its consequences
F. To understand the difficulties in dismantling the war system
G. To understand the need for considered judgment toward responsible action

A. Definitions

(Day 1) — Begin by asking what comes to mind at the mention of the words "war" and "peace." Use chalkboard for two lists.

Question 1 — Definition of the term *War*:
    (a) "War is a legally recognized and accepted mode for the violent (usually lethal) resolution of issues between groups."
    (b) "War is the final stage of diplomacy."
    (c) "War is organized group violence."
Question 2 — Definition of the term *Peace*:
    (a) "Negative" peace — absence of organized violence.
    (b) "Positive" peace — a pattern of cooperation and integration.
Distribute copies of definitions (see below) and discuss.

> *Peace:* Social Science has uncovered more knowledge about war than about peace, just as psychology probably has yielded more insights into negative deviance (such as mental illness) than into positive deviance (such as creativity). Unfortunately, studies tend to be focused on wars as units of analysis rather than on periods of peace, and there is a tendency to define peace simply as "non-war." Thus, peace thinking has had a tendency to become utopian and to be oriented into the future; it has been speculative and value contaminated rather than analytical and empirical. It is conceivable that this might change if research were to be focused more on peace than on war.

Two concepts of peace should be distinguished: negative peace defined as the absence of organized violence between major human groups as nations, but also between racial and ethnic groups because of the magnitude that can be reached by internal wars; and positive peace defined as a pattern of cooperation and integration between major human groups. Absence of violence should not be confused with absence of conflict; violence may occur without conflict, and conflict may be solved by means of non-violent mechanisms. . . . *(Encyclopedia of Social Science*, Vol. 11, p. 487)

War: organized group violence.

Negative peace: no violence but no other form of interaction.

Positive peace: some cooperation interspersed with occasional outbreaks of violence.

Unqualified peace: absence of violence combined with a pattern of cooperation.

The Various Differences of Peace: Approaches to peace differ depending upon how the term "peace" is defined. The Pentagon, under the motto "Peace is our profession,"[1] works toward its definition of peace with the policy of deterrence. Quite different is the UN working toward its definition of peace through *collective security*. In the UN Charter, note the four purposes of the UN.

B. Background Causes of 20th Century Wars

Show or project transparency[2] (T.P.-1) "Some 20th Century Wars" and ask Question 3.

Question 3 — What are the background causes for 20th century wars?

Probe for responses, acknowledging the same, and continue the inquiry in a one-page written report for Day 2. Each student should write on at least one war. Sources of information should be included.

(Day 2) — Hear reports for half of the period; then, before collecting the papers, project TP-2 over TP-1 and seek approval of this minimal wording. Aim for understanding of all terms and examples of each. Any additions like "Intervention"? (Note Manual, Item I, provides instructions for playing the simulation game "Intervention," a dynamic form related to Question 3. Consider its use in part of a period).

C. Humankind's Efforts to Peace

More on this later, but for now project TP-3, "Efforts to Peace," over

---

[1]This motto was coined by the Strategic Air Command — Ed.

[2]The transparencies are not reproduced here. They are available from the project — Ed.

TP-1 and 2. Distribute explanatory sheet (Appendix, Item 3 [available in complete curriculum manual]). Note: On the right-hand margin, Bilateral Negotiation might well replace Summitry. Distribute text booklet "World Military and Social Expenditure, 1984" (hereafter WMSE) and assign reading pp. 3, 5–9 on "Militarism." Significant facts and thoughts should be entered in student notebooks.

D. The Nature of Nuclear War

(Day 3) — Film "The War Game" (Nuclear Attack on England). Warning — possibility of emotional reactions. (See Manual, Item II.) Assign: Write a paper on your reactions to the film.

(Day 4) — Discuss reactions to the film and begin to deal with this next segment of the unit.

E. The Arms Race: Nature, Costs, and Consequences

In-class reading and explanation of WMSE, pp. 10–13, "The Nuclear Race," and from fold-out, pp. 41–43. Assign unfinished reading and this: List 3–5 subquestions, broadly related to E above, which you see as required study. Also invite clippings, articles, etc. At this junction, we now should have some answers to Question 4.

Question 4 — What is the apparent nature of Nuclear Warfare?

(Day 5) — Review assigned reading. Hear samples of subquestions. Then collect same for teacher's review and possible incorporation into the unit. We anticipate that one subquestion will be Question 5.

Question 5 — Who is ahead in the Arms Race — The U.S. or the U.S.S.R.?
Distribute the following:
1. For Day 6 — "Is the U.S. really No. 2?" [Appendix, Item 4, available from the project]
2. For Day 7 — The booklet "Soviet Military Power: Questions and Answers." (See also Manual, Item IV, "Monitor.")

(Day 6) — Review assigned readings and help students with questions on same. Ask for tentative vote on Question 5. Distribute "Soviet Military Power: Questions and Answers," and finish the period with in-class reading. Assign remainder for Day 7.

(Day 7) — Review assigned reading and take a second vote on Question 5.

Have students summarize the related data or arguments in their note-
books. On the chalkboard and in notebook, write Question 6.

Question 6 — What are some economic-social consequences of the arms
    race? To the world? To the U.S.A.?
    This little-discussed question is an ongoing study which might well
    begin at tonight's dinner table, be developed on the chalkboard tomorrow,
    then continued with related readings over Days 8 and 9 and possibly 10.

(Day 8) — Probe for answers to Question 6 and list them on chalkboard and
in notebooks. Then begin assigned reading from:
    1. WMSE, pp. 18–21, on "Economics-Social Decline." Notebook sum-
       maries should include details under at least these 4 "answers."
       a. Inflation
       b. Unemployment
       c. Income inequality
       d. Social neglect
    2. Whenever the class is ready, show excerpts from the WNET pro-
       gram, *Pentagon, Inc* (Appendix, Item 5).
       Assign: Write a page or two on the proposition "The Pentagon
       should administer a National Public Works Program." List argu-
       ments for and against.

(Day 9) — Continue the work of Day 8. Before collecting homework paper,
ask for a consensus on the proposition.

    Distribute "Do you know what your tax dollar buys?" (Appendix, Item
    6). Assign the question for Day 10 along with a review of Questions 3
    through 6.

(Day 10) — Review day for take-home, open-book test — topic/question to be
distributed at close of period. Due back to teacher in 2 or 3 days.
Choice of topics:
    1. Your thoughts and attitudes on "War is . . ."
    2. How would you vote on the current congressional resolution? (Ap-
       pendix, Item 7). Show your comprehension of the subject as you
       present your reasons.

F. The Evolution of the War System

(Day 11) — Note: (1) Because students have rarely studied war as an institu-
tion, the methodology used in this segment is less inquiry and more

substantive—teacher explanation and student note taking. (2) The subject is organized war, not conflict or violence. (3) If a student suggests that the answer to the lead question is "human nature," remind him or her that psychologists differ on such a claim.

Project TP-4, "The Evolution of the War System," and ask the lead question posed on the transparency ("Throughout history, man has fought: Why?"). It is likely that responses will draw upon our earlier study on the causes of 20th century wars. Point out that while such a listing is useful, our attention now is on different matters. Project TP-5 or TP-4 but cover all the content in red except #1. The idea is to uncover each succeeding concept along with the explanation. (15 minutes)

Now project TP-7, "Dismantling the War System," over TP-5. (We can expect some derisive laughter at our naivete. Nevertheless, probe for responses before adding TP-8.)

G. Difficulties in Dismantling the War System

However desirable and reasonable the concepts of TP-8 may be, it is certain that progress along such lines must include consideration of questions such as Question 7.

Question 7—What changes in attitudes, policies, and programs plus institutions are necessary in order to dismantle the war system? What personal, national, and international changes?

Assign: Think about Question 7.

(Day 12)—For some help with Question 7, Project TP-6 and distribute explanatory sheet (Appendix, Item 8). Aim for student understanding and appreciation of all terms. Consider Question 9 in other aspects, i.e.,

a. Swords into ploughshares or tanks into subway cars.

b. Reapportioning world military and social expenditures.

c. Bilateral negotiations toward weapons control and reduction. (See WMSE, pp. 22–25)

d. Can (or could) the UN help?

Distribute booklet "Improving the UN's Peacekeeping Capacity" and assign reading and note taking for discussion during the next two days.

(Days 13 & 14)—Discussion of main ideas in assigned booklet. Collect tests if still out. Teacher appraisal for possible use on last day.

Write on the chalkboard the final objective of this unit:

H. To Form Considered Judgments Toward Responsible Actions

Question 8 — What can we/I do about the War-Peace Problem?

(Day 15) — Summaries, consensus, answers to Question 8.

Collect the three booklets. Ask students to write a brief appraisal of the War-Peace Unit of Study. Finally distribute "Disarmament: The Social Aspects" (Appendix, Item 9) for students to check the number that most closely agrees with their present point of view.
Teacher may wish to have students return their copy of "Objectives" (Appendix, Item 1) on which each shows a self-evaluation on achievement. Do so by ascribing a number 1–5 (low to high) after each of the objectives.

Social Structures and Social Justice: Analysis and Action

This curriculum collection places an emphasis on problem analysis and the development of a sense of agency or capacity to take action in the face of the problems. The Leaven materials were designed by a group of Catholic women religious to promote both understanding and agency. The "Introduction" to the twelve-unit curriculum succinctly summarizes its purposes and approach.

Leaven hopes its members will experience a sense of participation in the movement that will enable them to act freely and creatively in their own world:
- By gaining an understanding of their own reality
- By realizing that they share joys, griefs, sufferings, and hopes with others in the world
- By developing skills to analyze their situation
- By designing or participating in actions which are aimed at effectively changing systems or situations harmful to people
- By acting in response to local and global issues with members of the movement and other interested persons
- By being a source of encouragement, power, and support for others in the movement and beyond it, and by forming relationships that will provide a sense of hope
- By seeing Leaven as a way to participate in the creation of a more just world

The Leaven units will help the participants share their own story
and reflect on their own reality to analyze what goes beyond the
interpersonal and to link local and global issues. They will be encouraged to join existing networks and to take actions for justice.
[*Introduction to the Leaven Materials*, 1984, p. 2]

The following extract provides an explanation of the Leaven framework for
structural analysis. Structural analysis is a significant method through which
to penetrate the causes of institutional (i.e., structural) violence and to gain an
understanding of the requirements for social justice (i.e., positive peace).

The units in the Leaven curriculum are:

1. Leaven Changes
2. Human Rights
3. Poverty and Affluence
4. United States Culture in the 1980s
5. Conflict Management through Listening
6. Racism: Two Americas
7. War and Peace
8. Structural Analysis
9. Sexism and Human Liberation
10. Global Limits
11. Change in a Democratic Society
12. Leaven Alive!

SELECTION 29
The Leaven Materials

Entrant: The Sisters of Mercy of the Union
Address: 1320 Fenwick Lane #610, Silver Spring, MD 20910
Grade Level: Secondary/adult
Department: Religious studies, sociology, social studies, government, social
    justice, and retreat programs
Concepts: How change, especially structural change, is made in a democrat-
    ic society; reflection on experience; structural analysis; action compo-
    nent
Topics:

Change	War and Peace
Human Rights	Structural Analysis
Poverty/Affluence	Sexism
United States Culture	Environment

Conflict   Change in a Democracy
Racism

Materials: Twelve self-contained units in Spanish or English. Bibliography
and resources available in each unit.
Instructional Methods:
Information presented
Reflection on information and experience proposed
Analysis made
Dialogue elicited
Action suggested
Cognitive Objectives:
Gain new information
Acquire new understanding of own reality
Develop skills in analyzing own situation
Participate in some change activity
Link local and global issues
Affective Objectives:
Realize that one shares joys, griefs, sufferings and hopes with others in
the world
Be a source of encouragement, power and support for others
Choose to exercise power and rights to change
Choose some actions for change
See what one does as participation in transformation of the world

LEVELS OF CHANGE

Change takes place on three levels of our reality.

1. *Personal*—individual, within the person.
2. *Interpersonal*—social, between and among persons.
3. *Structural*—societal, the ways persons are organized into societies,
   systems, governments.

The LEAVEN logo with its three concentric circles helps us to imagine
three levels of our reality.

1. The innermost circle represents personal reality—within the self, or between the self and God.
2. The next circle represents interpersonal reality—the relationship of the self to all persons in the family, job, neighborhood, or social situation.
3. The outer circle represents societal or structural reality—a level of which we are becoming newly conscious. On this level we relate to persons we do not meet personally.

Understanding structural reality helps us to understand how we relate to all others—through the structures to which we belong, relating to the structures to which others belong. Society itself can be viewed as a structure. Again structural reality can be viewed as the ways people are organized into societies, systems, governments, institutions, patterns, and cultures. We relate structurally to all peoples, those we do not meet as well as those we do meet.

Some examples of change on these levels of reality are:

Personal

I now do twenty minutes of Transcendental Meditation every day.
I learned some carpentry skills last summer.
I think differently about the draft now that I [am of age].

Interpersonal

My relationship with my [parents] improved when we both learned to listen to each other.
Tension at work between my boss and me has lessened since we both took a workshop in conflict management.
After listening to my neighbor's point of view, I joined him in welcoming neighbors of a different ethnic group to our block.

Structural

Demonstrations of public opinion in the United States have caused the administration to revise its defense policy.
The J. P. Stevens boycott has been called off now that the workers may vote to join the union.
My letter, along with thousands of others, probably had an effect on Congress' extending the Voting Rights Act.

Think about how change takes place on each of these levels:

Personal—by conversion (personal decision)
Interpersonal—by influence (we can influence one another by forgiveness, words, and example)
Structural—by power (groups of people can work together to change policies and the way things are organized)

Think of, and share one occasion when you saw change on each of these levels:

Personal: _____

Interpersonal: _____

Structural: _____

Infusion: Affecting the Entire Curriculum

Should peace education be subject specific, or should it pervade the curriculum? This question describes a significant tension in the field. The former approach may result in its being so compartmentalized that it is reduced to "just another subject." The latter carries the possibility of its being so "watered down" that the relevant knowledge is not adequately presented.

A comprehensive, sequential approach to peace education would involve both approaches. The infusion method as it has been adapted to global studies and peace education by JAPEC, the Justice and Peace Education Council (see Resource Organizations), is probably the most effective mechanism for such a comprehensive approach. The program of the Academy of St. Joseph is an example of the JAPEC infusion model.

As it infuses peace and justice concepts into the entire curriculum of the ninth through twelfth grades, the program introduces significant portions of basic information on major global issues.

This program requires the cooperation of an entire faculty and a commitment of a full day or two for infusion training. However, the great advantage, as is evident in St. Joseph's infusion program, is that aside from this cooperation and commitment, little retraining is needed and no curriculum redesign should be necessary. Any school can adapt infusion.

SELECTION 30
Education with a Global Perspective

Entrant: Sister Joan Larkin, CSJ

School: Academy of St. Joseph, Brentwood Road, Brentwood, NY 11717

Grade Level: 9–12

Subject: Integrated into entire curriculum with special emphasis in social studies, language, literature, science and religion classes.

Concepts: Community building — interdependence; multicultural understanding — global awareness; human dignity — social justice.

Topics: World hunger, human rights, global connections, peace, environmental concerns.

Materials: Standard curricula and various supplementary items mainly from Global Perspectives in Education, Inc. [see Resource Organizations — Ed.].

Instructional Methods:

1. Large group presentations — assemblies, prayer services, films, guest lecturers
2. Small-group discussions and classroom lessons
3. Projects — Oxfam, Thanksgiving baskets, letter writing to lawmakers, heritage map and UN flag displays, concerts
4. Special programs — Curriculum Day and Philosophy Day

Cognitive objectives:

A recognition of the interdependent nature of the world's political, economic, and social systems

An understanding and appreciation of basic human commonalities and differences

An awareness of how perceptions, values, and priorities differ among various cultures

The development of skills that will enable individuals to respond creatively to local, national, and international events and participate effectively at those levels

Affective objectives: To alter the school climate so that there is a visible commitment to the values of peace and justice; in particular:

a. To encourage faculty research, awareness, and support of such values
b. To provide experiences in critical thinking and values clarification
c. To develop the "Self-management Skills" of Global Education relative to attitudes

INFUSION PROGRAM AND PROCESS

School Goals

> *Curriculum*: To infuse the concepts of global education into all disciplines — to broaden students' vision.
>
> *School Climate*: To foster a more Christian school climate, visibly committed to the values of peace and justice.

Project Structure

> *Curriculum Committee*: Examines course outlines; develops specific objectives and learning experiences for various subject areas.
>
> *Theme Committee*: Develops overall plan for year; develops teacher in-service ideas; plans special events.
>
> *Department Goals*: Departments develop their own respective goals.
>
> *Monthly Focus*: Topics are selected for special emphasis throughout the school each month.
>
> *Teachers Plan*: Each teacher develops an individual performance plan and action plan.
>
> *Evaluation and New Plan*: Curriculum committee will review results at the end of each semester and plan new activities and topics for the next semester.

EXAMPLES

Foreign Language Department Goals

Curriculum goal. To infuse the concepts of global education into all disciplines. In keeping with our philosophy, we hope to increase the student's awareness of the many communities of which she is a member; we further hope to help her realize her responsibility to each.

Goal for year. To strive for an appreciation of values, culture, human universality, and an understanding of differences among groups and nations.

Individual Teacher Performance Plan

Goal. To acquaint students with the variety of cultures among Spanish-speaking people through:

Classroom study of various Spanish-speaking areas
Use of films and slides, projects and exhibits
Pen-pal exchange program
Field trips to museums, restaurants, etc.
Use of magazines and newspapers from Spanish-speaking countries

Indicators of achievement.   Program will be assessed through:

Student performance
Course evaluations
Team sharing
Classroom observation

Individual Teacher Action Plan

Teachers should make lists of what they plan to do in order to achieve each aspect of their performance goals. As the year progresses, the process of ongoing evaluation will enable the teacher to refine, clarify, or add ideas.

Focus of the Months

October.   Community: Philosophy Day — Student-faculty discussions on topic of responsibility to the many communities of which we are members.

November.   World Hunger: School participation in the Oxfam Fast; Thanksgiving baskets for the local community.

December.   Human Rights: Use of Universal Declaration of Human Rights to guide the study of human rights. Guest speakers invited; rights violations explored; letters written to lawmakers and embassies; prayer services.

January.   Human Rights: Contest for students on their interpretations of human rights; categories of art, music or writing.

February.   Heritage: Flags of nations in main hall; world map with each student's heritage marked; prayer services for global understanding. Celebration of Curriculum Day — Global Pageant; lessons on foreign cultures and languages, on world economy and governments, on ecology, etc.

March.   Peace: Four week emphasis — peace with oneself, with one's family, within one's community, in the wider world. Use of materials from the Leaven Movement and Educators for Social Responsibility.

April.   Ecology: New life — plantings; Leaven discussions on change; environmental projects; nuclear awareness on fortieth anniversary of atomic bombings; global implications-individual response.

May.   Summary: Review and evaluation.

Values Issues:
Individual Responsibility and Career Choice

An eleventh- and twelfth-grade physics course by Raymond Rogoway includes a values and ethics component by adding three films to the curriculum. These films, which convey a great deal of content about the development and potential consequences of nuclear weapons, serve as a basis for discussion of the ethical issues raised by weapons of mass destruction.

As they preview the films, teachers should develop questions to present to their class prior to showing the films; after the presentation, teachers should raise explicit questions about the specific choices made by those depicted in the films.

Teachers who find this approach suited to their goals will undoubtedly also find useful a booklet prepared by the Santa Barbara Study Group at the Institute for Theoretical Physics, University of California. It is entitled "Your Career and Nuclear Weapons: A Guide for Young Scientists and Engineers" and is available for $2.00 from the Peace Resource Center of Santa Barbara, 331 North Milpas #F, Santa Barbara, California 93103. At an age when many young people are making decisions about employment, military service, and/or the focus of future education, it is essential that schools offer opportunities for study and reflection on the social consequences of these choices.

SELECTION 31
The Social Responsibility of Science

Entrant: Raymond A. Rogoway
School: Independence High School, 1776 Educational Park Drive, San
    Jose, CA 95133

Grade Level: 11–12

Subject: Science/Physics

Concepts:

1. Career choices may in the sciences involve work which will have a major impact on society. Therefore, choices must be made consciously balancing individual and group needs with societal needs.
2. Values which may be easy to "take on" need to be tested.
3. Work assignments need to be examined for their impact upon society.

Topics: Nuclear war, weapons research, priorities of social structures.

Materials:

1. "The Day After Trinity," PBS TV program
2. "The Last Epidemic," Physicians for Social Responsibility videotape
3. "Testament," TV program

Note: Films shown in order given.

Instructional Methods:

1. Pre-discussion of careers, values, and impact of career on society
2. Viewing of videos
3. Post-discussion of emotions, feelings
4. Written answers to questions

Cognitive Objectives: The student shall be able to:

1. Perceive possible societal impacts of his/her career choice
2. Understand the potential direction of nuclear buildup
3. Understand that personal values may conflict with each other

Affective Objectives: The student shall be able to:

1. Give two conflicting values affecting self and society and make a conscious, thought-out, informed choice between the two
2. Project the consequences of nuclear warfare upon self and society

TEST FOR SOCIAL RESPONSIBILITY OF SCIENCE UNIT

Answer all of the following questions. Justify and explain your answers; yes or no by itself is not sufficient. Your answers will not be graded upon your opinions but upon the depth of explanation, logic, and your defense of your opinions.

These three questions will not be graded. They are for evaluation of the films. Please answer fully and explain your answers.

1. What was your response to "The Day After Trinity?" What feelings, ideas and/or emotions did it bring up?

2. Answer the above question for "The Last Epidemic."

3. Answer the above question for "Testament."

These questions will be graded.

1. Assume you have graduated from college and are now a professional, working full-time in your career. Would you ever work on a project that you knew would eventually kill or harm people?

2. Rank order, in terms of *importance* (whatever that means to you), the following list. Place the most important first and the least important last. Justify your choices.

World, Self, United States, Birth Country, School, Parents, Brothers and/or Sisters, Community.

3. Under what conditions, if any, should nuclear weapons be used?

4. Who is responsible for the deaths caused by weapons of war? The *scientists* and *engineers* who develop, create and invent them; the *workers* who build and test them; the *military officers* who decide when and where to use them; the *soldiers* who use them; the *government*; the *civilian population* that supports the war; *you*? (More than one answer is acceptable; justify each.)

5. If a person is working on a war-related project, should the government have a right to invade his or her privacy in the name of security? What level or amount of privacy should such a person have? What things should the government not do when keeping such a person under observation?

6. Do you think that nuclear war is preventable? How?

7. Do you believe that you could survive a nuclear war? Do you believe the world could survive a nuclear war? Give answers for both questions.

8. Assume that you have decided not to ever work on projects that will cause death or injury to people. You have been out of school for 3 years. You are now married and have a 10-month-old child. Your spouse cannot find a job and you were out of work for 18 months. You have now been employed for 6 months at a new company. There is a high unemployment and there were no jobs in your field available right now other than the one you have. Your supervisor comes in and transfers you to a project that will be used by the military to destroy people. What would you do?

Multicultural Understanding:
Local Community as Global Paradigm

An apparent assumption of much multicultural education for peace is that cross-national or global cultural differences relate more to the concerns of peace education than local or subnational differences do. While the inclusion of study of the world's cultures is essential to education for global citizenship, the elements of conflict and injustice related to cultural difference are usually more readily evident at the local and national levels. Indeed, cultural conflict within national borders now pervades the world and gives rise to a disturbing level of local violence. In some communities longstanding ethnic rivalries have been exacerbated by recent political events, and refugees from poverty, war, and oppression have introduced cultural diversity where homogeneity has been the norm. The local manifestations of cross-cultural differences are thus essential subject matter for peace education.

The problems and processes of integrating new, frequently rural, immigrants into urban society is one of the major motivations of the curriculum of Sister Sheila Campbell of Mt. St. Ursula Academy in a multi-ethnic New York community. While her curriculum does not deal with the newer waves of immigrants, it does deal with groups between whom there have been significant misunderstandings and conflicts, and its approach would be applicable to other groups. For example, the literature of Africa, Asia, and Latin America could be taught in the context of the heritage of recent immigrants.

This curriculum might also be complemented by Leaven materials (Selection 29) to show how cultural conflict is related to structural inequalities.

SELECTION 32
Immigrant Literature

Entrant: Sister Sheila Campbell
School: Mt. St. Ursala Academy, 330 Bedford Park Blvd., Bronx, NY 10458
Grade: 12
Department: English
Concepts: Multicultural understanding and acceptance on the part of multicultural students
Topics: 5 major ethnic groups of New York City: Italian-Americans, Irish-Americans, Black Americans, Puerto Rican Americans, Jewish Americans
Instructional Methods: An introductory, independent unit constructed around three themes: Family, Dreams, Self-Discovery in Ethnic Literature

COURSE OBJECTIVES

A. Identify the major thrust or thrusts for course (broad objectives which indicate a focus)
   1. To read a broad spectrum of ethnic literature in a thematically structured introductory unit
   2. To study the historical background of the 5 major immigrant groups of New York City: Jews, Irish, Italians, Blacks, and Puerto Ricans

3. To see the interrelationship of history and literature
4. To discover that ethnic literature has universal themes as well
5. To experience the living situations and culture of the groups by outside classroom activities

B. Ultimate Outcomes
   1. Knowledge or information to be learned:
      a. Historical background of 5 major groups
      b. Universal themes and ethnic themes of the literature
      c. Prejudice's roots and self-discovery of one's own prejudices
   2. Attitudes to be developed:
      a. Openness to new understanding of different ethnic groups
      b. Willingness to identify one's prejudices
      c. Identification with universality of the ethnic experience
   3. Skills to be taught:
      a. Reading for depth of meaning
      b. Essay writing reflecting above insights
      c. Poetry analysis

COURSE OUTLINE

A. Content
   1. Study of a wide variety of ethnic groups in a six-week introductory unit shaped around the themes of dreams, family, and self-discovery
   2. Study of the historical background of each of the 5 major immigrant groups
   3. Study of a representative number of literary pieces of each of the immigrant groups

B. Suggested Activities
   1. Sharing, through discussion, of insights into one's own ethnic group and those of others
   2. Personal reflection essays
   3. Outside classroom projects that give insight into the lived experience of each group

C. Methodology
   1. Lecture for historical background
   2. Reading days
   3. Small and large group discussion of study guide questions on the literature
   4. Written analytic essays, personal reflection essays, creative "essays" that capture the reality of the literature with quotes and photographs or other creative formats such as letters
   5. Oral sharing of outside projects by students
   6. A/V experiences

MATERIALS

A. Textbooks
   1. *A Gathering of Ghetto Writers* (Miller) N.Y.U. Press
   2. *Speaking for Ourselves* (Faderman) Scott Foresman
   3. *I/You We/They* (Farrell) Scott Foresman
   4. Each group's longer works — either in whole or part:
        Jews: *The Chosen* (Potok)
        Italians: *A View from the Bridge* (Miller); *Christ in Concrete* (DiDonato)
        Irish: *Studs Lonigan* (Farrell); *Long Day's Journey into Night* (O'Neill)
        Blacks: *Raisin in the Sun* (Hansberry); *I Know Why the Caged Bird Sings* (Angelou)
        Puerto Ricans: *Down These Mean Streets* (Thomas); *The Ox Cart* (Marques)
B. A/V Equipment
   1. For each group: history of that group
   2. General: "Prejudice in Literature"
   3. Videocassettes: *The Chosen, Raisin in the Sun, I Know Why the Caged Bird Sings, Puerto Rican History, Arthur Miller.*
C. Supplementary Activities
   1. Current articles as found by students or brought in by the teacher.
   2. Group experience of plays such as Lorraine Hansberry's *To Be Young Gifted and Black*, Arthur Miller's *A View from the Bridge*.
   3. Group experience of an ethnic group visiting Arthur Avenue, "Little Italy" in the Bronx, or having a lecture on a particular ethnicity by an outside speaker.
   4. Outside projects where each student writes up a non-print experience of an ethnic group and shares it with the class.

Art for Peace: Learning to See and to Show

One of the richest, still largely untapped resource areas for peace education is art. Visual art, in particular, is a rich medium through which students can express what is and what could be. Photographs and cartoons depicting the actual experiences of war and injustice and the politics that produce them, the painting, sculptures, weavings, and other works of art that interpret experiences—these are grist for the curricular mill. Education in the arts and education through the arts should be an integral part of peace education.

Students can learn much of the history of warfare and human struggle in great paintings such as Goya's on the Napoleonic wars and Picasso's "Guernica," to note the possibilities of the art of only one country. They can also learn much about how to express visions of what could be by studying architectural models or folk art such as the images stitched and painted on the "Pentagon Ribbon." Folk art and fine art alike provide a dimension of what is at stake in war, and what may be gained in peace, that textbooks, discussions, and simulations even at their best can never reveal.

Through art students can also articulate and share their own visions and feelings, frequently so difficult to put into words, especially for the young still struggling with understanding emotions and the mastery of language. By viewing art, learning how to see it and what to look for, they can come to understand others' visions and feelings.

Such lessons are embodied in "Disarming Images: Art for Nuclear Disarmament," prepared for an exhibition at the New York State Museum by Sharon Kolodny, Museum Instructor of the New York State Education Department. Teachers can apply this curriculum to any collection of art depicting war.

SELECTION 33
Disarming Images: Art for Nuclear Disarmament Education

Entrant: Sharon Kolodny
Institution: Museum Education Office, New York State Museum Cultural Education Center, Empire State Plaza, Albany, NY 12230
Grade Level: Curriculum was designed for elementary and secondary level, primarily 3rd grade and above.
Department: Interdisciplinary approach used in working with the corresponding art exhibit and preparing the resource packet.
Concepts:
    A. Art is a reflection of our society.
    B. Artists can make a statement through their art.
    C. The nuclear issue is a complex and interdisciplinary topic.
    D. People are concerned about this issue, with some preferring deterrence and others prefer disarmament.
Topics: Analysis of art, background information on nuclear energy and the arms race, suggested pre and post visit activities for the classroom, and a bibliography and resource list of organizations (for those who desire further study of the topics).
Instructional Methods: Conflict resolution, reading, discussion, etc., were utilized for the exhibit's lesson plan. Curriculum guide was designed to give teachers the necessary background information, skills, and sug-

gested classroom activities in order to make them feel less wary of the exhibit and the topic.

Cognitive Objectives:

How to analyze an art piece and reach conclusions about society, the artist's statement, etc.

That the nuclear issue is complex and involves sciences, history, art, morals, etc.

Affective Objectives:

To help students realize that everyone wants peace, just that the methods differ on how to achieve this goal.

That students should keep an open mind, realizing that it is a complex issue.

That students have the responsibility to do their own thinking.

INTRODUCTION

Art throughout the ages has incorporated political and social issues. Egyptian pharaohs, Roman emperors, and Napoleon all used art to support their power structures. Art gives us not just records of the way people looked and lived in any period of time, but how they *felt*. It is this tie to the emotions that makes the experience of an exhibit like "Disarming Images: Art for Nuclear Disarmament" both meaningful and difficult.

We present here some examples of artists and artwork dealing with controversial subject matter, including examples from this show. With these we suggest an outline of discussion techniques that will enable you to act as art critics, to stand back from the work briefly in order to see more clearly how the artists has created the emotional reaction we get from the work. [The complete unit provides a glossary, not reproduced here, to help those unfamiliar with discussions of art to see what peculiarly art-related meanings may be attached to ordinary household words. Slides of art works, which are not included in the unit, may be purchased or made — Ed.]

NOTE: Do not share the title, artist's name, or facts about the period/subject until after students have come up with their own interpretations.

DISCUSSION OUTLINES

Two-Dimensional Artwork

Part I: Description of the subject matter.   In this portion of the discussion avoid making interpretive or evaluative comments. Stick to actual, observable facts. For example, you may refer to a "bright-red" shape, but not to a "blood-red" shape.

1. What do you see in the picture?
2. Describe the main images.

Part II: Technical analysis.   Once again, avoid making interpretive or evaluative comments. These questions may be considered in whatever order seems appropriate to the piece in question and the group discussing it.

1. Describe the lines and shapes that you see. Are they exaggerated or distorted? Are they repeated? Do they create a pattern or texture?
2. Describe the colors and textures the artist has used.
3. Is this a complex or simple arrangement of lines, shapes, and colors? How is the work balanced?
4. Describe the size relationships.
5. Is there a single point of emphasis or several points that fight for attention (tension points)?
6. Describe the implied movement in the artwork. What lines and shapes lead your eye around the piece and to the point of emphasis?
7. Do you see examples of depth in the artwork? Are there overlapping shapes? Did the artists use changes in light or size (perspective) to indicate depth?

Part III: Interpretation.   Now you can share your "looks like"/"feels like" reactions to the artwork. Keep in mind that all interpretations must be supported by visual evidence.

Part IV: Post-script.   After all the possibilities of feeling and meaning have been discussed, let everyone know the title and artist and any other background information you may know. You may want to ask some additional questions at this point such as whether this new information changes their initial interpretation or why the artist succeeded or failed to get his message across.

Three-Dimensional Artwork

Part I: Description of the subject matter.   In this portion of the discussion, avoid making interpretive or evaluative comments. Stick to actual, observable facts.

1. What do you see in this object?
2. Describe the main images.
3. What materials did the artist use to create this?

Part II: Technical analysis.   Once again, avoid making interpretive or evaluative comments.

1. Describe the lines and forms that you see. Are they exaggerated or
   distorted? Are they repeated?
2. Describe the colors that are used.
3. Describe the way the forms create negative space.
4. Describe the implied movement (what leads your eye around the
   piece and what makes you want to see the other side?).
5. Identify any planes that may be important to the piece. Are they
   flat? curved? concave? convex? rough? smooth?

Part III: Interpretation.   Now you can share your "looks like"/"feels
like" reactions to the artwork. Keep in mind that all interpretations must be
supported by visual evidence.

Part IV: Post-script.   After all the possibilities of feeling and meaning
have been discussed, let everyone know the title and artist and any other
background information you may know. You may want to ask some additional questions at this point such as whether this new information changes
their initial interpretation or why the artist succeeded or failed to get his
message across.

SAMPLE DISCUSSION
Guernica by Pablo Picasso

Parts I and II: Follow the procedures described in the Discussion Outline for Description of the Subject and Technical Analysis.

Part III: Interpretation.   Share your "looks like"/"feels like" reactions
to this painting. Keep in mind that all interpretations must be supported by
visual evidence.

a. What do you think is happening here?
b. What feelings do you think the artist is trying to convey?
c. If this painting had sound, what do you think you might hear?
d. Does the choice of color have any particular effect?
e. How do you think the artist felt about the subject he painted?
f. Was the artist trying to convey any particular ideas?
g. What is the mood of the work?

Part IV: Post-script.   Share the title, artist and background with the group. As a final question you may want to ask what political or social concerns might an artist address today (or students can research this). The following background information could be given for *Guernica*:

The Spanish Civil War occurred between 1936 and 1939. The Nationalists, aided by planes from Germany and Italy, rose up against the existing government in a war that lasted 32 months, devastated the country's economy, and cost an estimated 1,000,000 lives. The end of the war brought Generalissimo Franco to power as a dictator.

In April, 1937, Guernica, an undefended Basque town, was destroyed in an air raid by Nazi planes in the service of Franco.

The painting *Guernica* has been described as an impassioned, compassionate indictment of violence.

Affective Approaches: War Stories

Story telling and theater performance have an especially rich potential for affective peace education. Dramatic performances based on readings from major works of literature or historic accounts can provide information while opening possibilities for exploring many other dimensions and implications. Such a presentation, from selection of the subject matter through design of sets, costumes, and make-up, and all other stages and processes of a dramatic production, can initiate much learning about "how it was" or "how it might be," not as a "historic" event but as a human experience. It is the human experience of war that, at least for Americans, is the hardest aspect for peace education to deal with.

Teachers might consider such activities as a way of introducing or culminating a unit of study. They can also be useful as a means of communicating to the rest of the school what classes in peace education have been learning. They can certainly enrich and enliven schoolwide programs and/or the use of infusion.

Kathe Ana of Tatterhood Farm, a private school, offers one example of this approach. "Stories of Hiroshima/Reader's Theater" is an ideal culminating exercise for a study of nuclear weapons, or of literature on Hiroshima or the history of World War II. The basic technique, however, can be applied to the history or literature of any war or any experience of violence or human oppression. Because of this possibility it is included among the curricula for Grades 10–12. However, it might also be adapted for lower grades.

SELECTION 34
Stories of Hiroshima/Reader's Theater

Entrant: Kathe Ana
Institution: Tatterhood Farm, Rt. 2, Pulaski, WI 54162
Grade Level: 5th–college
Subject: Theater/language arts
Concepts: It is important to hear the stories of the past in order to make a
   new story for the future.
Topics: Sharing stories, acting, writing stories from the experiences of people.
Materials: If the Reader's Theater is used with elementary students, books
   such as *Hiroshima, No Pika, The Butter Battle Book*, and *Sadako*
   could be used. For older grades, the elementary books plus *Home B/4
   Morning*, by Linda Van Devanter. A cassette tape of "Sadako and 1,000
   Paper Cranes" is available for $7.00 from Kathe Ana, Rt. 2, Pulaski,
   WI 54162.
Instructional Methods: Theater arts; discussion of experiences; reading
   aloud with expression.
Cognitive Objectives: Learning to pace a public performance.
Affective Objectives:
   Sharing stories, learning to feel the experiences of others.
   Understanding that people from other cultures share our aches and
      pains, desires and loves.
   Each selection of the Reader's Theater can lead to a broader discussion
      of *who* is affected by war, who "starts" war, winning/losing.

SOME THOUGHTS ON PERFORMANCE OF THIS READER'S THEATER

The stories used in this program are of real people from several wars.
The intent is to use various dramatic techniques, voice, dialect, gesture,
simple costuming, to draw people into the stories. This will allow every
individual to feel a small portion of the pain of war. No one escapes injury
in a war! No matter how far physically removed from a war experience, we
are affected.

The Reader's Theater can be used in tandem telling, single-person nar-
ration, even on a much expanded level; it is appropriate for full theater
production. Other visuals such as slides, films, dance, musicians, photos,
can be added for a full program on this story experience.

The program you plan need only be limited by your imagination, your
area of expertise, and the time allowed. However simple the production, it is
still effective.

This program was conceived by Kathe Ana, Storyteller. It was written and performed by Lee Bock, Storyteller, and Kathe Ana for public commemorations on Hiroshima Day in Green Bay, Menominee, and Milwaukee, WI.

Seeing the Possibilities: War Is Not Inevitable

The explanation of alternative endings to scripts and stories is an excellent way to introduce students to the concepts of multiple alternatives and alternative futures and an appropriate ending for a peace education curriculum guide. Having students propose different endings than those provided or offering an audience several endings from which to choose also makes for a more participatory and involving learning process. Teachers who use *The Butter Battle Book* with some of the lower grades will find it especially adaptable to this technique. The selection that follows is an ending one educator composed when presenting *The Butter Battle Book* to an audience of adult educators. This ending by Charlene Gleazer was not a survey submission. Her experience in using the alternative ending was recounted at the 1985 Teachers College International Institute on Peace Education, where many peace educators studied together to prepare themselves to help students to envision and work for a peaceful world.

SELECTION 35
How It Might Have Ended

Author: Charlene Gleazer

NEW VERSES FOR *THE BUTTER BATTLE BOOK*, BY DR. SEUSS

But at that very moment
A Yook came around
Advancing by tip-toe
With his eyes on the ground.

And also a Zook
Was standing quite tall
To see what was happening
Over the wall.

When the Yook sneaked around
For a much better look
His down-buttered bread
Collided with Zook!

Startled — amazed —
Unable to speak,
They saw they'd created
An edible freak.

Butter-side up
And Butter-side down
Went smoothly together
With hardly a sound.

They liked this new thing
Its success was a cinch
I think we should call it
A Zooky-Yooky Sandwich.

They called to their brothers
Who came with their bread
Each made a sandwich
Just like they said.

Divided in half
Each had a share
Which butter-side up?
We really don't care.

They broke down the wall
No longer divided
All of their bread
Is butter *in*-sided.

That ends the story
As told in our books
Of the Big Butter Battle
'Tween the Yooks and the Zooks.

You've seen how it ended
With nary a sputter
That awful, terrible battle
Over how to eat butter.

Indeed what began
With Snickberry Switches
Has now ended happy
As we all eat sandwiches.

Recommended Curriculum Materials

While there are a number of very useful curricula now in distribution, we have found no one item, package, or set of materials that will provide an adequate basis for a comprehensive program of peace education. However, many of the materials currently available can be integrated into such a framework, and many can be used to complement and enrich those in this volume and other teacher-designed curricula. What follows is a list of critical annotations reviewing materials recommended for such purposes.

The materials are listed alphabetically by title. It should be noted as well that many of the sources noted here also contain annotated lists of teaching resources.

Children's Songs for a Friendly Planet (K–6), Evelyn Weiss, ed. 1986. Riverside Church Disarmament Program, 490 Riverside Drive, New York, NY 10027.

> This is a unique and varied collection of songs of peace, justice, and occasions of celebration from various cultures and points in history. Songs are a marvelous tool for including the celebrative in peace education, and, as Priscilla Prutzman of Children's Creative Response to Conflict points out, singing is a natural medium for building community in the classroom. Especially helpful is the way in which the theme of the peace hero is woven through the selections. Each song also is accompanied by commentary that offers significant aspects of peace history and some of the basic concepts of peace and justice. This book will be a great resource for anyone working with groups of 5- to 11-year-olds in schools or other settings.

Choices: A Unit on Conflict and Nuclear War, a project of Union of Concerned Scientists in cooperation with Massachusetts Teachers Association and National Education Association. 1983. Available from National Education Association, 1201 16th Street N.W., Washington, DC 20036. NEA Stock No. 1425-10. 144 pp.

> The Unit contains ten complete, well-planned lessons intended to raise "fundamental questions about conflict, war, and nuclear weapons" (p. 7). It emphasizes that the teacher need not be expert in the area and provides clear directions, procedures, actual material for the classroom, and statements of purpose for each lesson, so that the teacher can have confidence in initiating this classroom inquiry. It provides in the lessons and the extensive appendices most of the basic information about nuclear weapons and suggestions about handling the issues and controversies surrounding the weapons.
>
> A careful reading shows the material to stand up to most standards for curricula on controversial public issues. The emphasis, as indicated by the title,

is on decision making and developing critical capacity. In all these respects it is an excellent unit. In terms of its own intention, however, and in light of the central concerns of peace education identified in this guide, the unit does have some shortcomings. It does not deal with war as an institution; neither does it offer sufficient exploration of conflict as a complex, universal, and multi-level phenomenon. The main and almost exclusive emphasis is on nuclear weapons.

Creating the Caring, Capable Kid, by Linda K. Williams et al. Palomares & Associates, P.O. Box 1577, Spring Valley, CA 92077.

This is a unique curricular program that integrates a number of highly participatory learning approaches into an exploration of various forms of violence from vandalism to global hunger. The goals of the program "are to help the next generation of young ones to: develop empathy and compassion; recognize the real-life consequences of real-life acts of violence; . . . [and] communicate effectively to manage violence," among others.

The program comprises a set of units appropriate for elementary schools. Each unit includes an illustrated storybook with discussion questions, an audiocassette with sing-along songs and an accompanying booklet of lyrics and discussion questions, and an activity book of lesson plans, directions for Magic Circle discussions, and suggestions for additional resources.

Creating the Caring, Capable Kid is an excellent curriculum for teaching about violence, care, and responsibility in a way that relates to both the experience of children and the problems of the community and the world. It combines cognitive dimensions of problem focus with the affective methods of songs and stories in a holistic approach to the child as integrated person.

Creative Conflict Resolution: More than 200 Activities for Keeping Peace in the Classroom, by William J. Kriedler. 1984. Glenview, IL: Scott, Foresman & Company.

William J. Kriedler has developed an invaluable resource that should be in the library of every elementary teacher. The activities he describes have relevance to all classrooms, whether the teacher specifically intends to do peace education or not.

The 200 activities, all very well described, cover conceptual aspects of conflict and peacemaking, specific approaches to particular types of conflict, from student-student conflict to student-teacher conflict, and a whole range of specific skills developments.

The book not only provides specific learning experiences and teaching techniques; it also offers a sound philosophy for what is currently called "classroom management" in a humane and peacemaking way. It is written from the actual experience Mr. Kriedler has had in his own kindergarten and early grades teaching, and it reflects a profound concern for the integrity of the children and the problems and needs of the teachers as well as the students.

He has drawn most effectively on the pool of resources that currently exist and has selected particular activities from other excellent curricula, placing them in the specific experiential context with which the majority of teachers will most readily identify.

In using such broad resources, both curricular and theoretical, he provides a rich bibliography from which any teacher would be able to acquire every-thing—theoretical preparation as well as the practical tools—necessary for un-dertaking responsible teaching of conflict resolution. This book might well be classified as required reading for elementary peace educators and certainly is to be included in every library and resource collection being developed by schools concerned with teaching children to be peacemakers.

Creative Conflict Solving for Kids, by Fran Schmidt and Alice Friedman. 1985. Grace Contrino Abrams Peace Education Foundation, Inc., P.O. Box 19-1153, Mi-ami, FL 33139. 40 pp.

The curriculum, and the booklet that presents it, is as creative as the conflict-solving techniques it offers. Made up of 40 reproducible student worksheets, it is beautifully conceived and sensibly sequenced. It emphasizes cognitive under-standing of conflict processes and affective commitment to constructive conflict resolution, what the authors refer to as "win/win outcomes." It provides a full and well-reasoned rationale for the approach, specifies the conceptual base and learning objectives for each worksheet lesson, and provides clear procedural directions and indicators of possible results.

Teachers will find this useful for teaching about conflict in general and about the conflicts that involve students. It will also promote better understand-ing and handling of student-teacher conflicts.

Creative Conflict Solving for Kids makes an excellent complement to the *Repertoire of Peacemaking Skills* (see below).

Crossroads Quality of Life in a Nuclear World: A High School Science Curriculum, by Dan French and Connie Phillips. 1983. Jobs with Peace Education Task Force, 77 Summer Street, Room 111, Boston, MA 02110. (617) 451-3389. 88 pp.

The best of three units produced to introduce nuclear education into secondary school classrooms, this booklet is a complete ten-day curriculum for senior high school science classes. While it is especially suited to courses in physics and biology, it is very adaptable for use in social studies courses. It would be an ideal curriculum for peace education programs that combine or coordinate the study of nuclear weapons in both science and social studies and for courses that raise issues of ethics and social responsibility. In addition to clear and full coverage of the physical damages and the size of the areas to be affected by full-force destruction and radiation, the unit also covers biological and ecological effects of nuclear explosions. It provides an introduction to areas of international conflict and war, as well as to questions related to "civil defense" and "limited" nuclear war, the economic consequences of military spending, and options for national security. The unit emphasizes map, graph, and statistical skills. The section on weapons development needs to be supplemented by updated informa-tion, but overall the booklet is still excellent for current purposes.

Crossroads Quality of Life in a Nuclear World: A High School Social Studies Curric-ulum, by Dan French, Kathy Greley, Susan Markowitz, and Robin Zane. (See Above.) 1983. 80 pp.

This, too, is a ten-session curriculum; while in some few elements of its content it repeats material in the science curriculum, it generally complements and extends that material. Yet, it also stands well on its own as a separate curriculum.

The social studies unit emphasizes conflict, conflict resolution, U.S.-Soviet relations, the human experience of Hiroshima, and the possibilities for future uses of nuclear weapons. Like the science unit, it reviews where wars are currently being waged and where the weapons are located (these elements are somewhat out of date).

What is severely missed in this otherwise excellent curriculum is a consideration of alternative security policies and multiple policy options in a global perspective. Equally unfortunate is the lack of coverage of arms control and disarmament agreements and possibilities.

Crossroads Quality of Life in a Nuclear World: A High School English Curriculum, by Dan French, Kathy Greeley, Susan Markowtiz, and Robin Zane. (See Above.) 1983. 84 pp.

Like the other two units for science and social studies, the curriculum has excellent material, some of which is repetitive of the companion curricula. For its designated purpose, English courses, it is perhaps the weakest of the three units. There are poems to read and discuss and a few excerpts from literature and newspapers, but much of the emphasis is again on "the bomb," what it did and what it can do. The rich literature of war and peace and the many novels about nuclear weapons that could have been exploited to the advantage of this unit would have offered a whole new dimension to the field of nuclear education.

Development Education: An Approach to Peace Education, by Sissel Volan. A teaching unit on disarmament, development and the child. UNICEF School Series No. 6. New York: United Nations, 1980.

This is a very useful kit that will be especially helpful to teachers of junior high school early adolescents seeking to introduce concepts of positive peace. It begins with some notes and suggestions for teaching about conflict and then proceeds to explore the links among military expenditures, disarmament, and development. It offers a very succinct, clear definition and illustrative chart describing and explaining physical violence and structural violence. It contains, as well, a number of other charts and overhead projections. One very good one deals with arms control treaties, and there are several excellent cartoon drawings illustrating the development of weaponry and its targets. Wall charts are also included.

Dialogue, A Teaching Guide to Nuclear Issues, Educators for Social Responsibility. 1982. Available from Educators for Social Responsibility, 23 Garden Street, Cambridge, MA 02138. 269 pp.

This guide is a landmark publication in the nuclear education approach to peace education. It offers resources, suggestions, tools and techniques for all levels K–12 and provides useful directions about how to develop a program, work with the community, and deal with resistance. It is especially helpful in placing its curricular suggestions in a developmental context and in offering examples of the kinds of discussions that actually take place in classrooms. An extremely useful section for secondary teachers is the one on critical thinking (pp. 20–22), which outlines components and procedures of a teaching process.

The material for Grades 4–6 deals well with some general issues on war, but the secondary materials focus more on the nuclear issues and do not introduce a consideration of alternative security systems, an element deemed essential in the approach advocated by this guide; useful material on the Soviet Union is included. Each section contains extensive bibliographical material for use at the relevant grade level and very helpful listings of resource organizations.

Since this publication ESR has produced many new materials for the annual Days of Dialogue, each different and each in many ways even better than its predecessors.

Educating for Peace and Justice (7th ed.), Vol. 1, "National Dimension," James McGinnis, ed. 1985. The Institute for Peace and Justice, 4144 Lindell Blvd., St. Louis, MO 63108. 300 pp.

This, the first in an invaluable set of three volumes, reflects more than any other specific American curriculum the normative and conceptual approach to peace education, lending itself well to a comprehensive framework. The organization of the volume is conceptually structured and the materials it offers are problem centered. The core values of the approach and the materials are nonviolence and social justice. While it is essentially secular in its presentation, the perspective seems to be rooted in the present Catholic social imperative of "the option for the poor," which asserts that peace is inseparable from social justice.

It offers illuminating background readings for teachers, well-planned and carefully explained lessons and learning activities, and, perhaps most significantly, an explicit pedagogical philosophy the editor has labeled "mutual education." This methodology is totally consistent with the core values of peace and justice education. It takes into account and attempts to overcome those elements in current educational practices and institutions that are antithetical to the core values. A chart is offered contrasting mutual education with the extremes of authoritarian and permissive education.

The other volumes of this 7th edition are Vol. II, "Global Dimensions," and Vol. III, "Religious Dimensions." We recommend that Volumes I and II be included in the libraries of all schools involved in peace education.

Friendly Creatures Features: Puppet Shows & Conflict Resolution Workshops for Primary Grade Children, by Mary Finn and Rosemary Murray. Western New York Peace Center, 472 Emslie, Buffalo, NY 14212. (Guidebook) 150 pp. and ½" Videotape (50 min.).

This is a packaged program which emphasizes both values and skills. The tape features four puppet shows dealing with affirmation of human differences, developing feelings of caring and sharing, and community cooperation. The guidebook contains explicit directions for teaching procedures, learning exercises, and activities for twelve conflict-resolution workshops. The book comes in a packet with check sheets and references to other enriching musical resources. This is a resource that will provide the perfect how-to-do-it for highly motivated early and elementary grade teachers with little or no experience in peace education. (Note: This resource is well complemented by the *Songs of Peace Booklet* from the Riverside Church Disarmament Program.)

The Home Port Controversy: Source Book for an Inquiry Curriculum, Metropolitan Area Educators for Social Responsibility. 1984. Available from ESR/Metro 490 Riverside Drive, 17th Floor, New York, NY 10027.

This is a conceptually well designed curriculum that gives sources pro and con on the controversy over the stationing of U.S. Navy ships equipped with nuclear weapons in New York Harbor.

In three parts, it provides information, source material, and "teaching strategies." Its major objective is to develop the students' capacities to make their own judgments on this and similar issues. The techniques and procedures can be adapted to the development of judgment-making capacities in general. It will be useful to teachers who want to teach about this controversy and also to any who are looking for models upon which to base inquiry units about other issues and controversies.

Some students may have difficulty with the reading level of the original source materials. Excerpting and rewriting may be necessary for students who do not read at an adult level. (Note: ESR/Metro is the New York City chapter of ESR national, which has local chapters throughout the country.)

Infusion: An Approach to Education for Peace and Justice Within the Existing Curriculum, a manual designed and produced by the Justice/Peace Education Council (see Resource Organizations for address). 33 pp. with an appendix of 13 pp. $4.50 including postage.

"Infusion," says this manual, "implies pouring in something that gives new life or significance to the whole." The experience of the reviewer with this technique and reports from teachers who have used it certainly validate this definition.

The technique is one that does not require any significant change in the curriculum. What it inspires, however, is a change in the teacher, providing new lenses for looking at the curriculum so as to see opportunities to raise issues and questions that lead to student reflection on peace and justice concepts. It is primarily a conceptual approach that enables teachers to incorporate "justice and peace concepts, knowledge, skills, attitudes and activities into appropriate segments of the basic content of the curriculum. It consists of matching concepts and skills" (Introduction).

The manual provides the basic steps for learning and implementing the infusion approach, including a basic set of peace and justice concepts and sample lesson planning sheets. It also provides an excellent list of resources — curricular, bibliographic, and organizational.

Infusion is a very good first step into peace education and a way to make an entire school conscious of peace and justice concerns, as St. Joseph's Academy (Selection 30) did. It can, as well, set the stage for the introduction of many of the sample units and courses extracted in this guide.

A Manual on Nonviolence and Children, compiled and edited by Stephanie Judson. 1982. Available from Religious Society of Friends — Peace Committee 1977, 1515 Cherry Street, Philadelphia, PA 19102.

By now a "standard work" in peace education, this manual, like a number of the pioneering materials in peace education, is still a very important resource for early childhood and elementary education. It provides a rich array of learning activities, complete with explicit directions and comments on how a given approach has worked and/or what the teacher may expect. It contains excellent essays and narrative materials dealing with the central conceptual framework of the four value goals around which the curriculum is constructed: affirmation, sharing, nonviolent conflict resolution, and cooperative community. The manual is a wonderful mix of "how-to-do-it" and "why-to-do-it," with contents ranging from how to organize staff, conduct meetings, and plan programs to a great collection of cooperative games and an annotated list of "Books for Young People."

Produced by the Nonviolence and Children Program, the manual is intended to meet the program's goals, which are extremely reminiscent of those integral to this curriculum sampler:

1. To develop an atmosphere of affirmation
2. To create an atmosphere where feelings can be shared and respected
3. To build a sense of community, of mutual support and caring
4. To teach problem-solving skills
5. To share our sense of joy in life and in others

Milwaukee Public Schools Peace Studies Guides. Available from Milwaukee Public Schools, Media Center, P.O. Drawer 10K, 5225 West Vliet Street, Milwaukee, WI 53201-8210.

These guides constitute a K–12 peace studies curriculum that emphasizes conflict studies and the nuclear arms race. There are individual guides for kindergarten through Grade Six, each of which focuses on aspects of conflict resolution, based upon the same set of fundamental concepts. The middle school curriculum is based upon the study of current events. Using concepts of conflict resolution and problem solving, it moves the inquiry from the immediate classroom and community settings to the national and global arenas. The high school guide, "The Nuclear Arms Race," deals with the history and dynamics of the development of nuclear weapons in the light of the concepts of military and political dominance, collective security, arms control, political accommodation, and deterrence.

All the guides are rich in resource suggestions and well-constructed lesson plans built around objectives that include attitudes, skills, and awareness of global issues. Throughout there is an emphasis on cooperation and positive human relations. Educators wishing to adapt the guides to a comprehensive approach to peace education can complement these units with others that extend topics to other areas of positive peace as well as inquiry into war as an institution and into possibilities for alternative security systems.

Militarization, Security, and Peace Education, by Betty Reardon. Valley Forge, PA: United Ministries in Education. 1982. 93 pp. Available from COPRED (see Resource Organizations).

This is a six-session study and discussion guide for adult education. It has been used, as well, in teacher education courses as a basic introduction to the substance, approaches, and goals of peace education. It was designed to facilitate the introduction of peace education into elementary and secondary schools by informing and enlisting the support of the community.

Militarization offers a general introduction to peace education by outlining the skills and values to be developed and specifies the broad set of learning objectives that are integral to the comprehensive framework suggested in this guide. Each session is followed by review and discussion questions to assist in the reflective process necessary to prepare for undertaking action on behalf of peace education. It lists and categorizes resources for deeper and more extensive study. Most significantly, it offers specific action strategies and a general plan for the introduction of peace education into the schools. It would make a good companion to this guide.

Open Minds to Equality, by Nancy Schindewind and Ellen Davidson. Englewood Cliffs, NJ: Prentice-Hall, Inc., 1983.

This "sourcebook of learning activities to promote race, sex, class, and age equity," while not a peace education curriculum as such, deals with issues essential to the concept of positive human relationships, which this guide has designated as one of the core values pursued by peace education. It should certainly be included in any approach that focuses on human rights. The well-conceived and clearly described activities help elementary and middle school youngsters to understand and recognize common forms of prejudice and stereotypes, as well as to develop values based on universal human dignity and change behaviors accordingly. It also is designed to facilitate change on the part of teachers, helping them to preside over classrooms that exemplify equality, where "all students have a fair chance to learn and develop as persons" (p. 5).

Peace Trek. Ark Communications Institute, 250 Lafayette Circle, Suite 202, Lafayette, CA 94549. Write for prices of various other curriculum items. Poster, $14.95.

The *Peace Trek* poster is the visual basis for a series of learning activities that emphasize creativity and the imaging of alternative futures. Students should find these activities involving, challenging, and stimulating. They foster hopeful, joyous learning and hold the promise of opening minds to positive possibilities and releasing energies for the tasks of learning and acting for peace.

The activities designed to go with the poster include suggestions for what we have designated in this guide as the childhood stage of the elementary grades, the pre-adolescent stage of the middle grades, and the adolescent stage of secondary school.

These materials can be used to extend and complement the materials we selected as examples of curricula to develop imaginative and artistic skills.

PEN Peace Education Packet, COPRED. Available from COPRED (see Resource Organizations). 118 pp.

This "packet" is actually a bound booklet, an updated version of materials originally assembled about 1980 by the members of PEN, COPRED's Peace Education Network. The collection still stands up very well as a general introduction cum how-to-do-it handbook for peace education. It provides a good overview of the major components of the field, a variety of replicable teaching units, and a bibliography keyed to its main sections.

Like many of the materials that come from those who were involved in the field before the advent of "nuclear education," it takes a broader view of peace and peace education, embracing elements of both positive and negative peace. It divides the substance into four general areas: violence and war; institutional violence; global awareness; and alternative world futures. It is a very good tool for beginners.

People Have Rights! They Have Responsibilities, Too. A Study Guide for the Universal Declaration of Human Rights for the Use of Young Citizens. Center for Peace and Conflict Studies, Wayne State University, Detroit. 1980. 30 pp. Available from the Center (see Resource Organizations for address; Contact the Center in regard to their other materials).

This guide was prepared for the upper elementary and middle school grades. It is one of the few materials for this age level, indeed for any school grade, that focus specifically on the Universal Declaration of Human Rights. The Wayne State Center for Peace and Conflict Studies is to be especially commended for its continuous, systematic, and high-quality work on human rights curricula.

The guide begins with a very well presented simple and basic introduction to fundamental concepts of social order, law and rights, and the general history of legal protections of rights in Western nations. It establishes the connection between human rights and peace by identifying inequality and injustice as significant causes of war. Thus this booklet is an excellent introduction to some basic concepts of positive peace for children aged 9–12. It is as well a very useful tool for teaching about the responsibilities of citizenship because of its assertion of particular responsibilities related to specific rights.

The basic content of the guide is the Universal Declaration of Human Rights, which is restated in simple terms. Questions are posed to facilitate reflection on the conditions and problems related to each right. It separates the civil and political rights from the economic and social rights enumerated by the Declaration by designating them as "Rights to Fair Treatment and Greater Freedom" and "Rights to a Good Life"; it augments the rights with "Responsibilities of All People for Making These Goals Come True." It identifies specific areas of citizen responsibility for the future in the form of a description of the major international human rights conventions and covenants, a listing that, unfortunately, is in need of updating.

In a resource section the guide provides the actual text of the Declaration, a glossary, and a list of related curricula.

The Person and the Planet: A Curriculum Guide, by Florence Widertis. Available from the author, 3318 Gumwood Drive, Hyattsville, MD 20783. 47 pp.

Complemented by a brief but eclectic bibliography and resource list, this guide for a senior high school problems course is the only material of its kind discovered in the review of materials now in distribution. It grounds the students' inquiry in an attempt to develop self-understanding and the possibility for individual change, and it introduces concepts of higher consciousness as background for the study of global problems. The approach is largely based upon Robert Assagioli's theories of psychosynthesis.

It offers, as well, a clear step-by-step model for building a global problem unit. The model can be adapted to any problem and easily followed by classroom teachers with limited preparation in either global issues or curriculum development.

A Repertoire of Peacemaking Skills, by Susan Carpenter. 1977. Available from COPRED. 60 pp.

This handbook is still the best single resource for the development of learning objectives in the area of positive peace. Starting from the premise that structural violence is as dangerous a threat to peace as the physical violence of war is, the "Repertoire" sees the task of education as preparing students to be peacemakers. This action/agent-oriented approach to peace education asserts that we need to teach how to engage in the behaviors that make peace. It clearly indicates that peacemaking can be learned, and that educators can learn to teach it.

It is a sound work, not only well grounded theoretically and straightforward about its assumptions, but also imminently practical. It lists skills, provides methods for their development, and offers sample cases to demonstrate when and how they might be applied.

If a peace educator can obtain only one resource, this should be the one.

Resolving Conflict Creatively: A Teaching Guide for Grades Kindergarten through Six, Metropolitan Area Educators for Social Responsibility and the New York City Board of Education Division of Curriculum and Instruction. Available from ESR/Metro, 490 Riverside Drive, 17th Floor, New York, NY 10027.

Developed from a hands-on classroom teaching program—the Model Peace Education Program developed in New York City Community School District 15—this guide contains a range of lively teaching materials that implement and extend many of the concepts and methods in *Educating for Global Responsibility: Teacher-Designed Curricula for Peace Education, K–12*. In the draft form reviewed for inclusion here, it contains ten sections ranging from conceptual definitions of peace and conflict through skills and attitudes development such as conflict, communication, overcoming prejudice and celebrating differences, to imagining and envisioning positive global futures. Each section has clearly described teaching modules organized for grade levels K–6. It is an excellent companion volume to *Educating for Global Responsibility* for elementary school teachers seeking a wider repertoire of teaching methods for peace education. The fully revised draft should be available by fall 1988.

Science Education, unpublished materials available from the Teachers Clearinghouse for Science and Society Education, New Lincoln School, 210 East 77th Street, New York, NY 10017.

Three curricula from the Teachers Clearinghouse could be used separately or combined into a single unit or curriculum for senior high physics classes. Those wishing to include a fairly short unit in a syllabus covering other subjects might want to use *A Nuclear Physics Primer*, by Rodney Labreque of the Westminster School in Connecticut, which provides introductions to nuclear weapons. Barbara Hull's course, "Science and Values," which she developed at Samuel Gompers Vocational/Technical High School in the Bronx, New York, deals with nuclear weapons and nuclear energy. Richard Shanebrook's curriculum was designed for a college level course in mechanical engineering, but it can easily be adapted for senior high school courses in physics, science and technology, or science and social responsibility. It makes excellent use of a variety of media and provides a very good overview of the scientific and human history of the development of nuclear weapons. It concludes with consideration of contemporary issues of weapons development and nuclear war prevention.

These three physics curricula demonstrate one set of possibilities for peace education in the sciences. It should be noted, however, that physics is by no means the only science subject area appropriate for peace education; indeed, virtually all the other sciences taught in secondary school lend themselves to this endeavor.

Simpleton Story: A Fairy Tale for the Nuclear Age, by Liane Norman. Illustrations by Marie Norman. The Pittsburgh Peace Institute, 1139 Wightman St., Pittsburgh, PA 15217.

This is a charming fable that, in the course of an entertaining narrative story, uncovers issues of militarism, the Cold War, and civilian nonviolent resistance to nuclear weapons. It comes with a study guide that gives many suggestions for both imaginative learning activities and more analytic ones.

The booklet is one of various creative resources available from the Pittsburgh Peace Institute, which also offers opportunities for academic study of peace issues and practical training in nonviolence.

World Concerns and the United Nations: Model Teaching Units for Primary, Secondary, and Teacher Education, based on the work of participants in the U.N. Fellowship Programme for Educators and the UNESCO Associated Schools Project. New York: United Nations, 1983.

This collection of model teaching units, published in *World Concerns and the United Nations*, is infused with a decidedly global perspective, as attested by the fact that the units are derived primarily from United Nations sources. This thoroughly comprehensive collection includes all the major issues facing the human family as they are confronted by the United Nations. It is most multicultural in content and in its origin, having been produced by educators from various parts of the world who have spent a period of time in study and curriculum development work at the United Nations. These authors also are persons of practical experience whose recommendations and methodological examples are sound, practical, and readily transferrable to the classrooms for which they are recommended. It is a virtual treasure-trove of teaching resources for classroom teachers at all levels and should be required reading for teacher education courses that are preparing teachers for any area of global and/or international education.

Throughout the book there are wonderful illustrations and photographs, making the units come alive and providing teachers with concrete tools that can be directly adapted to particular lessons and classroom discussions. The units and the directions are extremely well designed; each begins with an opening summary of its content and objectives and the materials and time it requires. The procedures are clearly outlined and are varied with sufficient discretionary and optional possibilities to provide choice and encourage creativity on the part of the teacher. It is beautifully indexed, including references to United Nations documents and programs, and contains an appendix with a set of documents that are in and of themselves of inestimable value as a collection for any educator working in this area. In short, it might be viewed as a kind of bible for educators for peace and international understanding.

World Military and Social Expenditures, by Ruth Leger Sivard. World Priorities, P.O. Box 25140, Washington, DC 20007.

This annual report documents global expenditures on arms in a comparative framework that includes — and contrasts on a nation-by-nation basis — public expenditures on fundamental human needs such as health care, education, and housing. The most recent issue is accompanied by a study and discussion guide, making this uniquely significant work into an indispensible peace education curriculum material that is especially well suited to secondary school classrooms.

World Order Series, prepared by the Institute for World Order (now the World Policy Institute) and published by Random House, 1973. $1.00 each. Available from CO-PRED.

This series of four booklets for Grades 9–12 presents a number of global issues within a world order framework, emphasizing values and alternative international system models. Each contains narratives outlining the framework and describing relevant models of the international system. Each presents historical and hypothetical case material through which to study the system; the human rights booklet also contains actual news stories of cases of rights violations. The booklets are well illustrated with photographs and charts and contain ample pedagogic materials in the form of questions and activities. A sample of one activity from the series is to be found in Selection 21 in this guide.

The four titles indicate the themes of the booklets; *Peacekeeping, The Struggle for Human Rights, War Criminals, War Victims*, and *Beyond the Cold War*.

Bibliographies

International Security and Arms Control: Curriculum Materials Bibliography. Stanford Program on International and Cross-Cultural Education (SPICE), Room 200 Lou Henry Hoover Building, Stanford University, Stanford, CA 94305. 29 pp. $3.00.

This excellent bibliography contains succinct annotations of curriculum materials, textbooks, references, audio-visuals, articles on nuclear or peace education, and bibliographies and film catalogues. It is an invaluable resource for classroom teachers. SPICE produces and distributes a variety of curricular resources.

Peace Education, A Bibliography Focusing on Young Children. Written and edited by Rosmarie Greiner. Resource Center for Non Violence, 515 Broadway, Santa Cruz, CA 95060.

One- to three-line annotations describe over a hundred children's books categorized under the topics of self awareness, awareness of others, conflict resolution, love of nature, global awareness, and imagination. This bibliography will be extremely useful for parents and teachers seeking to guide children's readings according to fundamental peace and justice values.

Resources for Teaching About Peace/War. Global Perspectives in Education (GPE), 218 East 18th Street, New York, NY 10003.

This listing is heavily weighted toward nuclear issues, but is generally comprehensive. It is annotated specifically for the purposes of classroom teachers. It describes a variety of background readings and many useful curriculum materials, only a few of which are listed in this guide.

GPE has been for a number of years the main national resource organization in for global concerns. They offer a wide variety of materials and services.

World Order Values: Books and Audio-Visual Materials for Children and Youth, A Selected Bibliography, with a Preface by Saul Medlouitz. Center for Peace and Conflict Studies, Wayne State University, 5229 Case Avenue, Detroit, MI 48202.

This bibliography is organized under the categories of four of the values identified by the Institute for World Order as essential to the achievement of world peace. It provides books dealing with issues and topics related to peace, economic well-being, social justice, and ecological balance. The useful annotations help teachers to select readings appropriate to the various levels of education, from pre-school through secondary. The greatest number of selections are for the elementary and middle grades. It is helpfully cross-indexed by title, grade level, and subject area. An appendix contains an annotated listing of films, slide shows, and recordings. No prices or rentals are given for the books or films.

Resource Organizations

The following organizations produce and distribute peace education resources such as journals, newsletters, and study materials. More extensive and annotated lists of peace-related organizations are available from the Fund for Peace and Institute for Defense and Disarmament Studies. Many of the major religious denominations also distribute peace education material.

American Friends Service Committee (AFSC)
1501 Cherry Street
Philadelphia, PA 19102

Center for Peace and Conflict Resolution
Wayne State University
5229 Cass Avenue
Detroit, MI 48202

Concerned Educators Allied for a Safe Environment (CEASE)
17 Gerry Street
Cambridge, MA 02138

Consortium on Peace Research, Education and Development (CO-PRED)
c/o Center for Conflict Resolution
George Mason University
4400 University Dr.
Fairfax, VA 22030

Educators for Social Responsibility (ESR)
23 Garden Street
Cambridge, MA 02138

The Fund For Peace
345 East 46th Street
New York, NY 10017

Global Perspectives in Education, Inc.
45 John Street Suite 1200
New York, NY 10038

Institute for Defense and Disarmament Studies
2001 Beacon Street
Brookline, MA 02146

Institute for Peace and Justice
4144 Lindell #400
St. Louis, MO 63108

Intercommunity Center for Justice and Peace
20 Washington Square No.
New York, NY 10011

International Peace Research Association — Peace Education Council (IPRA/PEC)
Robin Burns
School of Education
LaProbe University
Bundoora, Victoria 3083
Australia

Jane Addams Peace Association
c/o WILPF
1213 Race Street
Philadelphia, PA 19107

Justice and Peace Education Council
20 Washington Square No.
New York, NY 10011

National Education Association
1210 Sixteenth St. NW
Washington, DC 20036

United Ministries
Peacemaking in Education Program
Box 171 Teachers College
Columbia University
New York, NY 10027

United Nations
The Department of Public Information
UN Secretariat Building
New York, NY 10017

Women's International League for
  Peace and Freedom
1213 Race Street
Philadelphia, PA 19107

World Council on Curriculum
  and Instruction (WCCI)
School of Education
Indiana University
Bloomington, IN 47450

World Disarmament Campaign
Department for Disarmament Affairs
UN Secretariat Building
New York, NY 10017

World Policy Institute
777 UN Plaza
New York, NY 10017

References

Diallo, D., & Reardon, B. (1981). The creation of a pedagogic institute of peace. In *Basic documents* (pp. 195–197). San Jose, Costa Rica: University for Peace.

Fraenkel, J., Carter, M., & Reardon, B. (1973). *Peacekeeping.* New York: Random House.

Galtung, J. (1984). *There are alternatives.* Chester Springs, PA: Dufour Editions.

Greene, M. (1985, November). *What happened to imagination.* Paper presented at Teachers College, Columbia University, New York.

Jacobson, W. (1982). A generalized approach to societal problems. *Science Education, 66*(5), 699–708.

Jacobson, W. (1984, February). *Why nuclear education.* Paper presented at the Second Annual Nuclear Issues Conference, New York.

Jacobson, W., Reardon, B., & Sloan, D. (1983). A conceptual framework for teaching about nuclear weapons. *Social Education, 47*(7), 475–479.

Johnson, R., & Johnson, D. W. (Eds.). (1984) *Structuring cooperative learning: Lesson plans for teachers.* Minneapolis, MN: Interaction Book Company.

Laor, R. (1976). *A competency based program for cooperating teachers in modeling behaviours designated to assist pupils in developing helping and caring values.* Unpublished doctoral dissertation, Teachers College, Columbia University, New York.

McGinnis, J., & McGinnis, K. (1981). *Parenting for peace and justice.* New York: Orbis Books.

Macy, J. R. (1983). *Despair and empowerment in a nuclear age.* New York: Random House.

Reardon, B. (1973). Transformations into peace and survival. In G. Henderson (Ed.), *Education for peace: Focus on mankind* (pp. 127–151). Washington, D.C.: Association for Supervision and Curriculum Development.

Reardon, B. (1982). *Militarization, security and peace education.* Valley Forge, PA: United Ministries in Education.

Reardon, B. (1985). *Sexism and the war system.* New York: Teachers College Press.

Reardon, B. (1988). *Comprehensive Peace Education: Educating for global responsibility.* New York: Teachers College Press.

Sharp, G. (1974). *Politics of nonviolent action.* Boston, MA: Porter Sargent.

Sommer, M. (1985). *Beyond the bomb.* Cambridge, MA: Expro Press.

Thorpe, G., & Reardon, B. (1971). Simulation and world order. *The High School Journal, 55*(2), 53–62.

Weston, B., Schwenninger, S., & Shamis, D. (1978). *Peace and world order studies.* New York: Institute for World Order.

INDEX
Subject Areas, Topics, Themes, and Approaches Utilized in the Curriculum Selections

NOTE: Numbers following entries refer to Selections, not pages. In general, Selections 1–4 are most appropriate for the early grade (K–3), Selections 5–11 for the later elementary grades (4–6), Selections 12–15 for junior high grades (7–9), and Selections 16–35 for senior high grades (10–12).